### When Grampa was a
# MOUNTIE

# When Grampa was a
# MOUNTIE

*More* **POLICING STORIES**
*from the* **BESTSELLING AUTHOR**
of *Policing the Fringe* and
*Tragedy on Jackass Mountain*

Charles Scheideman

151 Howe Street, Victoria BC Canada V8V 4K5
© 2014, Charles Scheideman.
All rights reserved.
Without limiting the rights under copyright reserved above, no part of this publication may be reproduced, stored in or introduced into a retrieval system, or transmitted, in any form or by any means (electronic, mechanical, photocopying, recording or otherwise), without the prior written permission of both the copyright owner and the publisher of this book.
All photos taken by the author unless otherwise indicated beside a photo.

*For rights information and bulk orders, please contact*
info@agiopublishing.com
*or go to*
www.agiopublishing.com

*When Grampa was a Mountie*
ISBN 978-1-927755-10-5 (paperback)
ISBN 978-1-927755-11-2 (ebook)

Cataloguing information available from
Library and Archives Canada.
Printed on acid-free paper.
Agio Publishing House is a socially responsible company, measuring success on a triple-bottom-line basis.
10 9 8 7 6 5 4 3 2 1

To

My wife Patricia

Our children, Howard, Sherry and Christopher

Our grandchildren, Jos, Guinness, Sandro

and twins Elizabeth and Jack.

And to all those with whom I worked

during my career.

# Contents

| | |
|---|---|
| The Duty of an RCMP Wife | 1 |
| Fishing Farwell Canyon | 15 |
| The Kersley Crash | 23 |
| Murder, He Said | 29 |
| Bank Robber | 35 |
| Murder on the Lytton Ferry | 46 |
| Fraser Canyon Avalanche | 53 |
| Alberni Tsunami | 57 |
| Coffee Creek Bluffs | 67 |
| Cougar | 74 |
| Anahim Lake Patrol | 79 |
| Archie and the Six-Toed Dog | 84 |
| Defence of Drunken Drivers | 93 |

| | |
|---|---|
| H.E.A.T. at Golden | 97 |
| Horses, For Better, For Worse, and For Moose Hunting | 103 |
| The Flying Forest Fire | 113 |
| Fly at One Hundred Yards | 121 |
| The Dirty Thirties Escaped Prisoner | 125 |
| Turkey Lessons | 130 |
| Hope Beyond Hope | 138 |
| Lytton Weatherman Forecasts Extreme Heat | 151 |
| The Cost of Our Canadian Charter of Rights & Freedoms | 156 |
| Quesnel Wine Making, Featuring Mrs. Franco and Her *Grappa* | 159 |
| The Fred Quilt Frame-up: two constables ensnared in a tangle of pent-up resentment and orchestrated lies | 165 |

# The Duty
# of an RCMP Wife

**The four of us** who made up my family were transferred from Lytton to Golden in the early spring of 1972. We were all excited about the move to the new location but none more than I; this move put me into a promotional opportunity and I would soon be a corporal. Golden was also on the Trans-Canada Highway but it was a considerably larger community than Lytton and I would be getting a break from Native policing which I had been very involved with for the past five years at Williams Lake and then Lytton.

Our transfer was one of those "end of the fiscal year" ones where we had to promise to have all the paper work in Victoria headquarters by March 31 to allow the costs of the transfer to be billed to some remaining funds from the old fiscal year budget. Another condition of our move was that we would occupy the attached married quarters at the Golden Detachment. We were not entirely thrilled about living in the same building where I would be working because we had heard many stories from other policemen about the frequent calls to return to work to deal with any unusual occurrences when there were only junior policemen on duty. Golden Detachment, like most others of that size, had a high percentage of young constables and over the next few months we gained a much deeper understanding of this mode of living and the frequent need to provide some guidance to the young guys in the steep portion of their learning curve. The most positive aspect of this police office living was the very reasonable rental costs that were automatically deducted from my pay cheques.

It would be later during our first year at Golden, after we had learned to live with the frequent interruptions and had actually accepted our detachment life, that we would be informed we would have to find other accommodations somewhere in the community. This move was required because of the rapid increase in our detachment manpower; the attached married quarters would be converted into additional office space.

Our children, Howard and Sherry, had both started school at Lytton (in kindergarten and grade one) so they were uprooted partway through the school year and off we went. Those two handled the transfer like the big adventure it was for them; they were soon into their new school and had a string of friends who they would

# THE DUTY OF AN RCMP WIFE

often bring home after classes were over. The new friends liked to visit because they soon learned Howard and Sherry lived in the police office – an interesting place to see. Another plus about going home after school with Sherry or Howard was that their mother was always there with some treats and an ear for all the exciting things that had happened during the school day.

Golden was a busy place. Our newly promoted sergeant, Barry Beaulac, was a keen and very dedicated policeman. He ran the detachment in a way that motivated us all to do our best in every situation. One of his favorite lines was "there is no need to ever be bored in Golden" as long as that highway is over there. There was no excuse to not be busy and thereby make your day into something interesting. He was very correct in that observation and because of it and our recently acquired Canadian Police Information Computer system, Golden Detachment became well known to many police units between Toronto and Vancouver – most recognized by the specialized units along that route who dealt with stolen vehicles, stolen property, and missing or wanted persons.

A day seldom went by without one of our people finding an occupied stolen car or some vehicle that had been flagged in connection with some criminal activities. Because of the rather isolated location of Golden a very large portion of the highway travelers would stop there for fuel and food. Wanted vehicles with no occupants were frequently identified in the parking lots of the eating places. A bit of a "cat and mouse" game usually resulted in the car thief or thieves taking their seats in the "hot car" once again. As soon as the criminals had clearly demonstrated their knowledge and possession of the vehicle, they would be rudely made aware of our attention and our unbending requirement to have them occupy some of our accommodations instead. There were very few if any of these people who demonstrated any appreciation to us and the Queen for their free accommodations.

A few weeks after we had moved to Golden and moved into the attached living quarters, one of our patrolling constables was waived down on the highway by a very upset middle aged man. The fellow told the constable that he had been robbed at knife point and the two perpetrators had driven away in his car after relieving him of his wallet and even the change from his pockets. The unusual twist to this man's story was that the two criminals were young women. The victim in this case told us that he had picked up the two girls as they were hitchhiking near Banff, Alberta. As was routine in such cases we were more than a bit suspicious of the man's motives for picking up these two but there seemed to be no indication that he had done or attempted anything more than to give them a lift. Road hardened policemen will automatically look at events like this man described and wonder if he had been thinking with the wrong head when he got involved with

## THE DUTY OF AN RCMP WIFE

these two in the first place. All this suspicion did not negate what the man told us about these two and the confirmed offences at that point were armed robbery and vehicle theft as a minimum.

The man had been left standing on the side of the road in the Kicking Horse River canyon about 15 kilometres east of Golden on the Trans-Canada Highway. The two perpetrators had carried on in the westerly direction that they had all been on before the robbery. The victim gave a good physical description of the two young women. He added that while neither of them seemed to be mentally handicapped, he was quite sure that neither one of them could be considered bright or mentally astute.

The location they had chosen to commit their armed robbery was another indication that neither was among "the sharpest knives in the drawer." They were on a roadway with no intersections for about 130 kilometres behind them and they were stuck on that road for another 15 kilometres before they reached the first and only alternate route in the next 160 kilometres. I had never given much thought to the best place to commit a robbery but 15 kilometres up the Kicking Horse River canyon from Golden would have been well beyond the very bottom of my preference list. The constable who found this poor fellow standing at the side of the road had just driven up the canyon from Golden and no doubt he had met the girls driving the man's car, among the heavy traffic only a short time before he was flagged down by the victim.

WHEN GRAMPA WAS A MOUNTIE

The information was radioed to our Golden office immediately and a patrolling constable began watching for the suspects along the highway. He was soon joined by two more patrol cars. One car drove west on the Trans-Canada Highway at high speed, assuming that the suspects would most likely stay on the main road. The other two men began a systematic search of the area within the town starting near the main highway. The search was re-directed within a few minutes when one of the policemen spotted the stolen car parked among the many customer cars at a popular eating establishment. The policeman drove by the stolen car as though he had not seen it. The possibility of the suspects getting into the car again was definitely a long shot, but strange things happen in the world of crime and dull or stupid offenders.

A frantic scramble began in our office to get someone out of uniform to have a look around inside the eating place. The policeman who had spotted the car had positioned himself so he could watch the car without being seen by the suspects, assuming that they were in the roadside restaurant. The other police units continued their patrols while watching for female pedestrians or hitchhikers.

In a very short time two girls came out of the café and hopped into the stolen car like they owned it. They were suddenly made aware of the fact that they had made a large mistake by stopping in Golden. The handcuffs were tight and uncomfortable and the

6

# THE DUTY OF AN RCMP WIFE

cops were not in the least bit interested in their story about borrowing the car from a friend. They soon heard the sound of the heavy steel-clad door of our holding cell as it slammed behind them.

Another interesting aspect of this strange story was that the two young ladies seemed so confident in their anonymity they had left all their belongings in the stolen car while they enjoyed their meals. If the policeman who spotted the car had stopped behind it in the parking lot, the two thieves may well have been forced to attempt their getaway with only the clothes they were wearing. This was just another indication of how much thought and planning these two had put into their criminal venture.

The two became our guests for a considerable number of days. We learned that they were from Eastern Canada and that they were long-time acquaintances and they had both been into previous brushes with the law but nothing as serious as the offences they were now facing. There were no holding facilities for females within a reasonable distance in British Columbia and there was no possibility, in those days, that they could be released on bail. Prisoners held in our cells for an extended time were always a problem but this situation was doubled because they were females. The law and the policy of the RCMP required that a female guard be on duty at all times when females were in custody.

My wife Patricia was drafted for this duty as a matron, guard, along with several other women from the community so that 24-hour coverage could be maintained. Pat had experienced this duty on a few previous occasions at Williams Lake and at Lytton but she saw immediately that these two were going to be much more of a challenge than her previous charges had been. She immediately set about trying to develop a rapport with the two prisoners, along with the other two ladies from the community who shared the difficult task of dealing with the two misfits. Their efforts were met with only sass and abuse. By the third day in custody the girls seemed to be mellowing a little and Pat had developed some communication with them; however, they were still mouthy and abusive to any and all who came in contact with them.

The overall conduct by these two clearly indicated that they should have been kept confined to the steel holding cage in the cell block room but as the days dragged by they were allowed out of their cage to enable them to get some exercise. The first experiments with allowing them out of the cage were done with only one at a time being given the "freedom" of the entire 12 by 12 foot room while the other remained locked in the cold steel cage which was inside the same room. The two "unruly bitches" actually seemed to appreciate being given this minimal freedom so they were soon allowed to have the cage door left open. Hindsight

# THE DUTY OF AN RCMP WIFE

being what it is we soon learned that these two "princesses" had suckered us all into allowing them out of the cage together. Pat had provided a deck of playing cards and some chalk from our home. They were then able to spread a blanket on the cell room concrete floor and play cards; they were still a hell of a long way from being trusted with a card table and chairs.

Pat was on duty in the morning of the first day that these two had access to the entire twelve by twelve foot cell room; she had taken their breakfast to them and collected the utensils after they had eaten. A check of the cell room showed all in order and Pat took her position in the adjacent office and made the required frequent checks through the tiny window in the cell room door.

The police building in Golden was likely about twenty years old at that time and the construction standards were not very demanding in those days. The cell block rooms were simply doubled dry-wall construction over wooden studs. There were beveled strips of trim wood nailed in place around the glass block window opening which allowed some outside light but no vision in either direction. The beveled wood trim strips were of the same wood material that was used as trim around windows in every wood-frame constructed home during that era.

Pat became aware of the sound of the continuous flushing of the toilet in the cell and went to see what was going on. She immediately found that the little window in the cell room door was completely blocked with wet toilet tissue and paper towel. Sounds from the room indicated that the two occupants were moving around continuously and they were making splashing sounds as they walked on the flooded floor. Another sound indicated that they had something in their possession that they were then pounding against the walls and the steel cell cage. Pat immediately called for help from the office staff; I was in the office at the time and rushed to the cell room door along with another of the men who happened to be there at the time.

We opened the cell room door and saw the two of them crouched near the flooding toilet. The two delightful maidens had shoved a blanket into the toilet and jammed the flush mechanism of the toilet so it flooded the room. They each had a section of the wood trim they had torn away from around the cell block window and they were holding these in a menacing stance. The wood strips had nails protruding from them and would have been a dangerous weapon had they been able to apply them to an unprepared person.

In the court rooms of today these two would enter a plea of insanity and would no doubt be successful. We had a more realistic assessment of such conduct in those days; we knew the two were completely aware of what they were doing but had learned from their previous experiences with law enforcement that they could get away with almost any sort of sub-human behaviour. We

## THE DUTY OF AN RCMP WIFE

had secured our service revolvers in the office as was required of all of us before entering a holding cell. As we shoved the door wide open and entered the cell we took a page from the *Dirty Harry* movies and advised them to, "Go ahead and make our day!" We followed immediately by advising them that they might get in a swing with their sticks but the scenario immediately following would be very painful for them. Obviously the two cops presented a very threatening vision to the girls; they put down their sticks and followed our detailed instructions. They were ordered to lie face down on the flooded floor with their hands behind them. Handcuffs and leg irons were applied so that they were shackled with their hands and feet intertwined. They were then gently dragged out and into the other smaller holding cell.

The flood was cleaned up and the window trim was replaced and secured in position by long screws rather than the standard finishing nails that had allowed the girls to easily pull it away from the wall. The two prisoners were kept locked in their cells in separate rooms for the duration of their stay with us. Fortunately they were sentenced within the next day or two and they were escorted away to serve their sentences in the facilities for women somewhere in the Vancouver area. Their final act of defiance had been a nuisance to us but it seemed to have brought the two prisoners to their senses. They both entered guilty pleas and were sentenced to sixty days in jail followed by one year of probation to be supervised by authorities in their home province of Ontario.

Within minutes of the sentencing hearing the two prisoners became the subject of our undivided attention. We made firm plans to get rid of them from Golden and get them to the provincial jail for women. The Province of British Columbia established the Deputy Sheriffs service the following year but at the time of these events, all prisoner escorts in the province were the responsibility of the police organization that had instigated the arrest or warrant. All the required paper work was completed with a priority. The two sweethearts were scheduled to be taken to Revelstoke the next morning on the first leg of their journey to jail. Pat was the scheduled matron on duty at the time of the prisoner escort to Revelstoke so her duty then required her to ride in the police car to Revelstoke and back. A young constable was selected from the shift to drive the car and convey the required paperwork and the bodies to Revelstoke, a distance of about 150 kilometres each way.

Pat was never a great fan of highway travel. She was very nervous in any vehicle and this condition became more of a problem in direct proportion to the volume of traffic on the road. She really did not want to make the long highway trip to Revelstoke and back but agreed to go in this case as it seemed to be a necessity of her temporary employment.

# THE DUTY OF AN RCMP WIFE

Unknown to us, the young constable who was selected to make the drive had been to a party the night before and he was more than a little bit short of sleep when he showed up for work that morning. The two prisoners were handcuffed together and placed in the back seat of the car and away the four of them went. Pat soon noticed that her driver was not completely alert and this added greatly to her anxiety. She was well beyond the condition that could be described as wide awake and frightened. About an hour into the drive she realized that the police car was too close to the centre line of the highway. A quick glance at the driver confirmed her worst fears: he had dozed off at the wheel. A shrill scream brought him back to reality with a jerk and he was able to take the appropriate corrective action and avoid a certain crash at highway speed. A brief and "to the point" discussion followed wherein Pat advised him that if he was not able to stay awake he must get off the road and a radio call would be made to have someone take over for him. The young constable was then wide awake and apologized repeatedly and pleaded to have the happening remain their secret. Pat agreed to this but made him completely aware that she would never ride in a vehicle with him as the driver again. The remainder of the drive to Revelstoke was accomplished without any similar events. The two prisoners were handed over to another police car from Kamloops to continue their journey to jail in the Vancouver area. My highly overstressed wife watched very closely as the police car made the return trip to Golden and home.

We heard no more of the two young prisoners but assumed they had returned to their home areas in the East after serving their time. The police and the probation authorities were often on different pages of the rule books in those times so we heard nothing of their doubtful conduct while they served their time and their terms of probation.

# Fishing
# Farwell Canyon

**My family and I** were transferred to Williams Lake in the spring of 1967; this was the beginning of my experience in the area of Native policing. My first posting at Nelson in the West Kootenay region had lasted nearly seven years and Native people are rare in that part of the province. I found myself in a steep learning curve to do with Native policing and the very different types of events that I would encounter as an almost daily occurrence. I had heard many stories from my workmates who had been in such areas but one is always a little inclined to think that many such stories should be taken with a "pinch of salt!"

I soon found that the "good old boys" with their hands-on experience had little or no need to exaggerate their stories. Those of us policemen who came to the Cariboo area soon learned the "art" of dealing with those Natives who had basically abandoned their rural reservation way of life and chose to become urbanized by taking up residence within the towns and cities of the region. The group who existed on the streets and back alleys of Williams Lake were known among the police and among themselves as the "Troopers." This group was a nuisance to the general population and the police through their constant alcohol abuse; their overpowering need for alcohol totally dominated their daily existence. Their constant intoxication often led to anti-social behaviors such as assaults, vandalism and traffic obstruction. They frequently suffered injuries; a day rarely went by that one or more of this drunken group was not rushed off to the local hospital by ambulance.

Fortunately the Troopers were not typical of the broader indigenous population. Most Natives from the surrounding area would only come to the town for shopping needs and they were as welcome and law-abiding as anyone else in the community. On their arrival these people busily went about their gathering of supplies and other needs, and they were soon headed back to their rural life. I found it interesting to visit with these people in Williams Lake and while out on rural patrols to learn about their way of life in the vast Chilcotin, one of the few remaining regions where they were still partially able to live close to nature as they had for many generations.

Some of the Chilcotin Natives told me about their annual

# FISHING FARWELL CANYON

fishing experience at a place known as Farwell Canyon. The Chilcotin River passes through the Farwell Canyon for its last few kilometres before plunging into the much larger and muddy Fraser River. Farwell Canyon is a deep water cut in the bedrock of the Chilcotin Plateau. The canyon walls are almost vertical throughout much of these few kilometres and people must use abundant caution in getting around near the river. I learned that the sockeye salmon made their annual spawning migration from the Pacific, up the Fraser River and then into the Chilcotin River around the end of July or during the first two weeks of August. The people relied on this abundant migration for their winter food supply now just as they had for hundreds or perhaps thousands of years. Some of the Natives invited me to watch their fishing activity, and recommended the river bridge across the Chilcotin River in Farwell Canyon as the ideal observation spot.

It was early in August that I found an excuse to make a patrol into the Chilcotin area and specifically to Farwell Canyon. As I came near the river I found a large Native camp. They had parked their trucks and campers and trailers in a draw that provided shelter from the wind and was close enough to the river fishing place that they could walk there easily. There were a few tents in the camp but the majority chose to use more modern accommodations. I was met and welcomed by some of the folks I had encountered in Williams Lake and we enjoyed a visit. They

## WHEN GRAMPA WAS A MOUNTIE

First Nations fishers using dip nets to catch salmon.

## FISHING FARWELL CANYON

told me their fishing had been somewhat "on and off" but quite productive in the overall. Some of the older Natives were tending drying racks where fish had been cut into strips and was being dried and smoked in the open air. We were invited to try some small samples of the partially cured fish, and it was delicious.

My partner and I parked the police car as close to the bridge as possible, and where we'd be able to watch for anyone who may have wanted to damage it. We knew that a few Natives harboured deep grudges against the Force, and might be tempted to vandalize an unattended cruiser. We then walked out onto the bridge deck. The river in the Farwell Canyon is in a deep and rock-walled gorge. The bridge is not long but it is very high above the water and provides an ideal spot to observe the Native fishing activities below. From the bridge deck we could see five or six men perched on narrow rock ledges just above the surging river. The fishermen each had a long fibreglass pole with an aluminum hoop on one end; the hoop was fitted with a nylon bag net very similar to a landing net commonly used to get line-caught fish into a boat. The net was dropped into the surging water at the farthest upstream spot that could be reached with the long pole handle and it was then swung slowly through the water in a downstream direction to the end of the fisherman's reach. This fishing method was known as "dip netting" and was illegal to everyone except Natives.

The turbulent water created a noise that did not allow any conversation among the men who were fishing. The Chilcotin River water is beautifully clear at that time of the year but the surging action in the canyon filled the water with tiny air bubbles that made the water opaque. This water condition did not allow the fishermen to see the fish but it also prevented the fish from seeing the fisherman.

In a short time we saw several fish deftly landed by the net-wielding fishermen below us. Some of the fishermen had built a small rock enclosure where they placed the fish they had caught; others used a burlap sack to hold their catch. As the fisherman swung his net downstream he could feel whenever a fish collided with his net – immediately he would twist the fibreglass pole to close the net and then pull it to the surface and deal with his catch.

As we watched the fishing activity we saw a Native boy about ten or twelve years old making his way along the canyon's steep rock wall. We were both concerned for the safety of this lad as a slip or fall would most likely put him into the surging water where he would almost certainly drown and the body may never be recovered. We wondered what reason there could be for this youth to be in such a dangerous place. The boy was making his way to a point above one of the fishermen where he would be on a rock ledge within reach of the upper end of the fibreglass pole as it was swept through the water. The roar of the passing

# FISHING FARWELL CANYON

water prevented the fisherman from hearing the boy above him on the ledge; his presence would only be known if the fisherman saw some movement or if some gravel was accidentally dislodged from the canyon wall.

The young fellow finally reached his objective where he steadied himself on the ledge and watched the pole of the dip net as it made a few passes near him. The next time the pole came by the lad reached out and hit the end of the pole with his open hand. The jolt was immediately noticed by the fisherman and he instantly assumed another fish had hit his net. He quickly twisted the fibreglass handle as he pulled the net to the surface where he was obviously baffled by the emptiness of the net. We were being treated to an obvious example of the Native sense of humour in action. The youth was clearly enjoying himself and he was able to fool the fisherman several times before he was noticed. Both the fisherman and the lad enjoyed a good laugh, and the boy then made his way to a safer place.

This experience was as close as I would ever come to seeing one of the traditional Native methods of gathering their sustenance. By overlooking the vehicles with campers and trailers and the modern day fishing equipment in use, we could have very well been observing a fishing venture that had taken place several hundred years prior to that day.

The original Chilcotin Natives were fortunate to control the area where this abundant fishery was an annual event. Having this resource may have brought about the aggressive historical reputation of these Natives; they would have needed to be able to vigorously defend their food source from all neighbouring tribes.

Before getting back to our patrol duty, we visited for a short time with some of the Natives in the camp area. They explained that before the white settlers arrived, they used wooden poles and netting woven of cedar bark strips. The fibreglass poles with nylon netting along with their clothing and camping equipment were all things that had been added in relatively recent times. By over-looking these things my partner and I were both glad to have taken the opportunity to see the fish harvest. It was such a healthy contrast to policing the Troopers back in town. These Natives were following in the footsteps of their ancestors and it certainly appeared that people of all generations were thoroughly enjoying the experience.

# The Kersley Crash

**It was early spring** in 1980 in the central Cariboo area around Quesnel, with new leaves producing the beautiful green that rapidly spread across the winter-dulled countryside. The weekend weather had been beautiful, a fact that had brought out more people than usual to enjoy the bar scene and other activities in the community. It was the time of the year that brings about Spring Fever, a renewal that definitely affects the attitude and judgment of all of us – for better or, in some sad case, for much worse.

A group of six teens from the little community of Kersley were enjoying a weekend of fun and foolishness; they had enjoyed a little beer but none of them were intoxicated. Three young men from a small mining operation near McLeese Lake were also enjoying some time off the job and they had set out to drive to Quesnel to see if they could find some action. They too

WHEN GRAMPA WAS A MOUNTIE

had been into the beer in a limited way but none of them were drunk. All nine were just feeling good and perhaps were a little more inclined to throw caution to the wind than they would have been without the liquor and the cheering effect of the beautiful spring weather. The road was clear and dry.

One of the group of teens from the local area had borrowed their family car for the evening; there had been no plans to go anywhere except to get them from home to home as they went about their visits. The car was a full-sized American-made sedan. The three young men from the local mine were in a full-sized pickup truck belonging to one of them.

Al was one of the constables on my watch; he had been scheduled to work until 2:00 a.m. and he was going about his work in a caring and conscientious manner as he always did. The town was beginning to quiet down so Al had come to the office to start the paperwork that always took up a lot of time at the end of each shift.

At 1:30 a.m. a very upset man called from a roadside pay-phone to say that he had just seen one of the most horrible vehicle crashes that he had ever heard of. The man described how a vehicle had passed him at very high speed and it had in a moment come into a head-on crash with another vehicle. The whole scene had then disappeared into a huge ball of fire. He had no idea how many people had been involved in the two vehicle head-on but he

# THE KERSLEY CRASH

told the police operator with certainty that there could not possibly be any survivors. Such incidents were known at that time and are still today referred to as "code black".

Al was immediately back in the patrol car and driving in full emergency mode to the reported scene. The police office dispatcher/guard called for an ambulance to attend the scene as a matter of routine. The town was still busy enough to occupy the other two on-duty constables so Al was "on his own." About eight or ten minutes of hard driving brought Al to where he could see a flickering glow on the night sky. He then knew he was about to go where no "right thinking" person would want to be.

The scene was unimaginable. The vehicles had met in the center of the road where both had been straddling the centre lines of the highway. Obviously the southbound car had been cutting a fairly abrupt curve to their left, travelling at a very excessive speed. The pickup truck was also travelling at very high speed and it seemed to have drifted partly across the centre lines, due again to its speed. At the moment of impact both vehicles had the highway centre line directly under the front center of each unit.

The two vehicles came together squarely and with such perfect alignment that at that moment they became one. The nine young lives were snuffed instantly. The huge momentum of the two vehicles was absorbed between them. The explosive impact had lifted both vehicles as a single unit to a height of about twenty feet above the road surface. The wreckage crashed back to the highway surface and came to rest within only a few yards of the initial impact. The impact had ruptured the gasoline tanks of both vehicles and the witness told us that the vehicles were still in their upward flight when they became a ball of fire. There can be nothing positive said for such a tragedy although in this case it was fairly obvious that none of the vehicle occupants were left to die in the fire.

At his first glance Al could clearly see that there were no survivors and he then clearly understood how the man who reported the crash could say with such certainty that no one was alive; he positioned the marked patrol car with the emergency lights in operation so that it provided maximum visibility around the curve to both sides of the crash. He placed incendiary flares on both sides of the scene and then stood by waiting for the fire to burn itself out. The ambulance crew arrived about that time but there was nothing that they could do.

The small rural community had a volunteer fire department which consisted of an old truck with a water tank and pumping equipment. A call was made through our office and the volunteers began to gather around the old truck; they arrived at the scene about thirty minutes after our police unit and the ambulance. The hell fire had subsided greatly by the time the fire truck arrived but they began the task of cooling the wreckage to allow access and

# THE KERSLEY CRASH

recovery of remains. The old truck carried a very limited amount of water that was applied to the fire in a very fine spray to avoid the total obliteration of the charred remains. The water tank of the truck was about empty when water began to pool in the melted and burned hole in the asphalt roadway. The thing was then cool enough to begin the next phase – the recovery of remains.

The volunteer firemen began their task with the typical care and dedication of such a group but as the fire slowed and they were able to see more clearly into the wreckage they began to realize that one of the vehicles was from their own community. One of the volunteer firemen was the father of one of the crash victims; he was removed from the scene in the ambulance.

At first Al was quite sure there had been a minimum of four persons involved but as he and the firemen gathered and sorted throughout the burned out vehicles they continually increased their count until by daylight they were sure they had a death count of nine. A second constable had come to the scene to assist when Al had radioed the office with details of what he was facing.

The little rural community of Kersley was devastated; there was hardly a home in the entire area that had not been directly affected. The three young men who had been in the other vehicle had come from a variety of locations around the province.

A policeman had to be cut from some very tough material in those times and Al was a prime example of this fact. If ever there was a cause for "post-traumatic stress disorder," this incident would have been a leader. Al's experience will no doubt have left some permanent scars but those of the unfortunate firefighter and father are unimaginable. PTSD as a malady was not acknowledged in that era. The most common advice available to a policeman who had experienced such a thing was "suck it up" and "get on with it."

# Murder, He Said

**Many success stories originated** with the installation of the CPIC computer at Golden Detachment in 1973. This was at a time when there were very few if any policemen or anyone else in Canada who knew anything about these miracle machines. We were told the keyboard on this new machine would allow us direct access to the entire police information data bank for the entire nation. We all stood around it and marveled at the potential of it. Our detachment commander at Golden was William Barry Beaulac, RCMP regimental number 18517, one of the finest police officers that I had the opportunity to work with during my entire career. This man became well known for his global thinking on the complicated subjects of policing in general, and the overall effect and purpose of each unit of a police organization. He was thrilled about the new equipment and could hardly wait for it to become operational.

## WHEN GRAMPA WAS A MOUNTIE

The installation was accompanied with a basic training course where all of the uniformed members and the clerical staff were introduced to the proper use of this equipment and told of the capabilities it had in the continuous fight to enforce the law. Barry immediately saw and eagerly accepted the potential for this new equipment – especially the importance it could have at a location like Golden where nearly every unit of traffic on the Trans-Canada Highway would make a brief stop for food and fuel. His motivated attitude about his job was spread to all those of us who worked at Golden; he would often say, "There is no reason to ever be bored or complacent about your work in Golden. If you are not busy at any time, just go to the highway and check a few vehicles. You will find something interesting to deal with and your work hours will seem to fly by." As usual he was "right on the money."

A totally opposite attitude was displayed by the detachment commander at a nearby unit on the Trans-Canada Highway. This man had always advised his detachment people to stay away from the highway: "All you get out there are problems that belong to some other police unit, and we sure as hell do not need that." A very interesting comparison was displayed between these two units; the validity and folly of each is abundantly clear.

Golden Detachment nearly always had some clients in our cells,or, as we referred to them, "guests of the Queen." This fact required that we would always have a civilian "prisoner guard"

## MURDER, HE SAID

on duty around the clock. The primary duty of these people was the safety and security of our prisoners but we arranged for them to be given basic training in the entry of inquiries into the CPIC computer system. The guards enjoyed this activity and were able to do queries on the computer yet still keep very close supervision on our cell occupants. The radio use and typing skills of our prisoner guards improved rapidly and their participation allowed another uniformed member to be out in the community we were there to serve.

The most obvious effect of this diligent application of our new computer was that Golden became known by police units over the entire span of Canada but most specifically on the Trans-Canada Highway between Vancouver and Toronto. A day seldom passed without some computer "hit" bringing a wanted person into the reach and grasp of the justice system. Our guards were pleased to participate in this way and they all enjoyed the challenge and the satisfaction when they "made a hit" on the computer.

One of our regular guards was a long time good citizen of the community. His health had deteriorated and he was no longer able to work at his regular job which required physical exertion. This man was very asthmatic, a condition which forced him to go about everything in a very slow and cautious manner. However he needed income and he genuinely enjoyed his participation and contribution to the policing of his community.

WHEN GRAMPA WAS A MOUNTIE

There was frequently a backlog of calls from the patrol cars when this man was on the radio and computer but we learned to live with it mainly because of the thorough and conscientious attitude he applied to every item that was called in by one of our patrolling policemen. I was in the office one evening preparing a report on some aspect of my job when I overheard the following radio conversation.

Two of our constables were going about their work around the community. Part of their work was to call in license plate numbers of vehicles they encountered or the name and details of any persons they encountered whom they did not recognize as a local resident. The following exchange took place over about ten minutes.

**Patrol Constable** – "Car 514 to Golden – can you run a name for me?"

**Office Guard** – *Some raspy breathing can be heard on the radio followed by:* "Go ahead 514." *A bit of raspy breathing followed until the radio carrier closed.*

**Patrol Constable** – [Then calls in the name and birth date of an older man.]

**Office Guard** – *Raspy breathing, then* "Stand by," followed by raspy breathing.

*Five or ten minutes pass until the radio carrier becomes active again and the raspy breathing can be clearly heard for*

# MURDER, HE SAID

*several seconds followed by:* "Ken – have you still got that guy with you?" *followed by a short session of raspy breathing.*

**Patrol Constable** – "No, but he was hitchhiking by the Husky service station on the highway. What have you got?"

**Office Guard** – *Raspy breathing.* "You better go back!" *followed by raspy breathing.*

*A few minutes pass before the Patrol Constable calls to say,* "I have him in sight again! What have you got?"

**Office Guard** – *Raspy breathing.* "Stand by – there is something on him here." *followed by a brief bit of raspy breathing.*

*A few more minutes pass until the radio carrier opens again.*

**Patrol Constable** – "Can you tell me what the entry is for?"

**Office Guard** – *Raspy breathing (a bit longer than normal).* "He's wanted for murder." *followed by more raspy breathing.*

**Patrol Constable** – "Holy shit! I'll bring him in!"

In a few minutes a marked police car pulls up behind the office where I am now standing to offer assistance. I can see a hunched and very sad looking old man in the back seat, tears streaming down his face. We brought him into the office where he repeated the confession he had blurted out when the constable came back to him on the highway. He told us how he and his (now dead) wife had gotten into some liquor and how everything went wrong and they got into a fight and he pushed her down the stairs. He then realized that she was dead and he tried to run away. He had hitchhiked about two hundred and fifty kilometres from his Alberta home to where he was standing by the highway when the constable had approached him and asked for his identification papers. At the time he was checked he claimed to have been trying to decide if he should continue his run-away or come to us.

The sad domestic assault had taken place only about twelve hours before we made the arrest at Golden. Without the new miracle of the CPIC computer there would have been no report of the incident for several days and the old fellow would have been left to his own devices. His conduct and attitude indicated to me that, if that had been the situation, the end result might well have been suicide.

Another CPIC hit had been accomplished but this one had a rather sad ending.

# Bank Robber

**Glen Garry Frazer was** born in Morden, Manitoba on August 30, 1934. Garry's father was employed as an agricultural representative for the Province of Manitoba; he worked with farmers to improve agricultural practices throughout that area. The Frazer family moved to Winnipeg in time for Garry to do his schooling there. After completing high school Garry found work he enjoyed with the Manitoba Forest Service and after one year on that job he decided to enter studies in forestry at the University of British Columbia. The first year of his studies went well but he began to feel overwhelmed by the fact he would need a minimum of three more years of studies before graduation. At the end of his first year of university studies he returned to Manitoba and joined the RCMP on April 30, 1954.

Garry and his troop mates from all over Canada were sent to the RCMP training establishment in Ottawa where they spent almost a full year. He was then transferred to British Columbia and he worked at Vancouver Town Station until he volunteered for the RCMP musical ride. He stayed with the musical ride for two years; during his first year the ride performed in the Eastern United States and they rode at the Winter Fair in Toronto. The highlight of his time with the musical ride came during his second year with their tour of the British Isles and their performances at the Edinburgh Tattoo.

After the musical ride Garry returned to the BC Lower Mainland area, stationed at Richmond. During the time Garry worked at Vancouver Town Station before going to the musical ride, he had met Kerry Langtry, a young lady who had recently graduated as a Registered Nurse from the Vancouver General Hospital training school. Their chance meeting was to become a life-long commitment.

In those years the RCMP was quite dependent on its ability to transfer their men on very short notice and at minimum cost. Married men were much more cumbersome and costly to move which resulted in a policy that no member could be married until he had completed five years of continuous service. This policy served the RCMP very well for many years but times and attitudes changed and their young men began to feel this policy was somewhat unfair. Pressure for change began to build and the Force realized their marriage policies were causing them to lose

# BANK ROBBER

many promising young men. To deal with this problem the Force established a policy that allowed their men to be married after three years of service on the condition they would accept a posting to a large municipal detachment.

Garry transferred to Burnaby early in 1958 and he and Kerry were married on April 11, 1958. Burnaby and Surrey were then and still are the largest municipal policing establishments of the RCMP in all of Canada.

Early in 1961 Garry, Kerry and their new baby daughter were transferred to Terrace, BC. Garry had eight years of police experience at that time and he was therefore the senior constable at Terrace Detachment.

On the morning of March 15, 1962 Garry and the sergeant in charge of the detachment were in the police office discussing the requirement for Garry to become "the man in charge" of the detachment while the sergeant would be away for an advanced training course of six weeks at Regina, Saskatchewan. During that conversation, a citizen came into the police office to say he had just seen a well known local woman go into the bank with a rifle. The woman who was reported to have the rifle in the bank was a "character" who had gained a reputation around the community through her odd conduct. This woman had no criminal history but she was rather unpredictable and seemed to enjoy doing strange stunts for no obvious reason. In the world

# WHEN GRAMPA WAS A MOUNTIE

of today this lady would be described as being "part of the local colour."

The bank was directly across the street from the police office so Garry walked over with the intent of asking this lady to remove herself and her firearm from the bank. As is so often the case, the information given to the police was very inaccurate. The person who had reported to the police had either been mistaken or he had received the information from someone else and vital facts were blurred or lost in the transfer. What had all the markings of another almost comical incident rapidly became a disaster.

The bank building had two sets of glass doors that formed a vestibule; there was no other exit or entrance to the business place. Just as Garry got inside the first doors, he could see a man standing behind a counter with a rifle in his hands. At that instant a shot was fired that shattered the second glass door and a large fragment of the bullet struck Garry in the abdomen and knocked him to the floor. The man fired four more shots in rapid succession. One of these bullets hit Garry just above the knee of his left leg. The intended targets of three of these shots are unknown but considering the confined area of the bank and the background of the man with the rifle it has to be considered miraculous that Garry survived. The rifle that the bank robber had just picked up that morning from a local hardware store was a military surplus weapon. It was a .303 British Lee-Enfield Mark III army model

## BANK ROBBER

very similar to those used by this man and his comrades in their daily duties as front line soldiers. Many of these rifles became surplus after the war and they were made available to the public at bargain prices. The ammunition the man had obtained was soft-nosed, hollow-point hunting type ammunition. The rifle used on that tragic day is still in the RCMP museum at Regina.

The man with the rifle was a local resident and well known by many of the citizens of Terrace. He had served in the army during the World War II and had become a victim of what was referred to in those times as "shell shock". Today his condition would be described as "post-traumatic stress disorder". The man had a wife and eight children and they were in constant financial difficulties due to him not being able to find and maintain full-time employment. No doubt the man was very familiar with the rifle he used in this crime however it seems he was in such a state of mind that he could not use it to its full and deadly potential – or he did not want to do that, although the first round he had fired would indicate he intended to kill.

Moments after the shots had been fired, the man attempted to leave the bank through the only access and egress where Garry lay wounded. Garry got to his feet and forcefully took the rifle from the man as he passed. He drew his service revolver but held fire because by then the man was running away. The self-control and cool headedness demonstrated by this severely wounded policeman at that moment are beyond comprehension. He considered the emergency over when he took possession of the rifle and he chose not to try to shoot the person who had, only moments before, attempted at least twice to kill him.

Immediately after the last shot had been fired, the local citizens and bank staff sprang into action. Some ran blindly away in terror. Others began to deal with the horrific emergency they were facing. Several local persons ran after the shooter and overpowered him a short distance from the bank where they held him until he was taken into police custody. People called for medical aid and an ambulance, and some tried to comfort Garry and reassure him as much as possible in his severe situation.

Later investigations showed the man had ordered the military surplus rifle and ammunition through a local hardware store and that he had waited for more than a week for the weapon to arrive. This would certainly indicate premeditation but his state of mind was also demonstrated by the fact that he had un-wrapped the rifle from the shipping container and left the wrapping, with his name and address, near the bank he intended to rob.

Dr. Robert Edmund Musgrave "Ted" Lee was the surgeon at the Terrace hospital and he was called to the scene of the shooting. Dr. Lee arrived very shortly after the shooting; he administered pain medication and worked very effectively to control the excessive blood loss. Dr. Lee followed the ambulance to the local

## BANK ROBBER

hospital where he immediately began surgery to treat the massive abdominal wound caused by the soft-point bullet. A tourniquet had been applied at the scene of the shooting to control the bleeding from the leg wound. The abdominal wound was very severe and it was the primary threat to life; so the full attention of all available medical people was applied to that aspect on arrival at the hospital. The first bullet had mushroomed and shattered passing through the plate glass door, before causing extensive damage in Garry's abdomen. Hours of surgical work were required to save his life. Garry and Kerry have great respect for the surgical skills of Dr. Lee and his assistants for their work on the day of the shooting; they both believe that Garry would not have survived the day without the tremendous efforts of these people under the very capable guidance of Dr. Lee. They were pleased that Dr. Lee lived to enjoy many good years of partial retirement in Victoria but they were saddened by the news of his passing on January 8, 2012.

Dr. Lee and his team of assistants worked non-stop well into the evening. By the time they were able to direct their attention to the secondary wound in Garry's leg, there was no possibility of saving the damaged limb – amputation was the only option available. The surgical team were nearing completion of their work on the abdominal wound when it became obvious there were still some particles of foreign matter in the wound area. They had to open the wound to remove some shrapnel missed on the first

# WHEN GRAMPA WAS A MOUNTIE

attempt. Fragments of the bullet had carried pieces of his clothing and his uniform deep into the wound.

As the news of the shooting spread through the community, many citizens came to the hospital to donate blood to help with the emergency. Kerry still recalls the line of people waiting to donate while she waited outside the operating room.

Fourteen days after the shooting, Garry was flown to Shaughnessy Hospital in Vancouver where there were better facilities to aid his recovery. A Canadian Forces Air Sea rescue aircraft was provided for the transfer; Garry and Kerry still recall the ride in the unpressurized aircraft as it skimmed along just over the ocean water off the west coast toward Vancouver.

Garry spent the following four months in the Vancouver hospital. Kerry and their daughter moved to Vancouver where they stayed with friends while Garry struggled with his recovery.

The man who shot him was a war veteran and no doubt was suffering from "post traumatic stress disorder" even though that condition was still unrecognized in those times. The bank robbery was his first venture into criminal activity and he had made a mess of it. He pleaded guilty to the charges of attempted murder and armed robbery, and was sentenced to fifteen years in prison.

RCMP regimental number 18624 Glen Garry Frazer was awarded the Commissioner's Commendation for bravery and promoted to the rank of corporal immediately after the shooting.

# BANK ROBBER

As his recovery progressed he returned to police work in an administrative capacity. The RCMP showed its appreciation by underwriting Garry's education; his recovery had progressed sufficiently well by September of 1962 that he resumed courses at the University of British Columbia, this time studying administration processes. During his summer breaks he worked at the Vancouver RCMP headquarters.

On April 8, 1963, Garry and Kerry were called to Ottawa for the presentation of the "George Medal" to Garry for his outstanding act of bravery and sound judgement on the day of the bank robbery. Garry's parents were also able to attend at the Ottawa ceremony. The presentation was made by Governor General The Right Honourable George Vanier. Vanier had lost a leg during his military service during World War One.

The George Medal originated in Britain during the Second World War when Britain was under heavy attack by enemy aircraft. The medal was awarded to both military and civilian persons for acts of outstanding gallantry during those terrible times which became known as the "Blitz". The George Medal is still awarded for acts of gallantry by the countries of the British Commonwealth for bravery and sound judgement.

In the fall of 1967 the Frazer family was transferred to Victoria where Garry worked at the BC RCMP headquarters. In the summer of 1969 they were moved to Ottawa where Garry was promoted to the rank of sergeant and then staff sergeant. In 1974 they returned to Victoria headquarters from where he retired to pension in 1983.

That horrible day was fifty-one years ago and Garry has struggled with the damage inflicted on him every day since then. Kerry tells of how Garry has refused to give way to his severe handicap. He will take on almost any challenge that life presents and he will do physical activities that perhaps he should not do. Kerry says she long ago learned to never suggest that Garry could not do some job or activity because he will simply get on with it and get it done in spite of his handicap. This characteristic of Glen Garry Frazer was clearly demonstrated in the doorway of that bank many years ago when he got to his feet in spite of two bullet wounds and forcefully took the rifle away from his assailant.

Today, Garry and Kerry have four children and three grand-children. Garry and his wife have miraculously overcome the bitterness that one would expect from the victims of such an experience. They recognized that the man responsible for their years of suffering was not in control of himself at the time, and they are philosophical about it all. I was somewhat surprised that Kerry refers to the original happening as the day of Garry's "accident". Discussion with her about this aspect led me to understand the validity of their choice of words. Most other descriptive language about the incident would only contribute to bitterness and hate,

## BANK ROBBER

and these two great people are far above that. Garry is glad of his decision to not shoot the man during their close encounter in the doorway of the bank. There is a very big man in Mr. Frazer's boot and a very heroic lady in Mrs. Frazer's shoes; the world would be a better place if there were more folks like these two.

# Murder
# on the Lytton Ferry

**Lytton was its typical** hot and sleepy place on this day in the summer of 1968. The police first became aware of a problem about noon, when a local citizen came to the RCMP office to advise that something was very wrong on the little cable ferry that crossed the Fraser River just north of Lytton. The complainant advised that the ferry had been stationary in the middle of the river for almost an hour; a situation that had not happened before. The man lived in a location where he could see the ferry from his living room window so we were quite convinced that his concern was genuine. Apparently no vehicles had approached to cross the river; and therefore the problem was not noticed until the observant man realized that something was wrong

An immediate patrol took only a few minutes to drive the two kilometres to the ferry landing on the Lytton side. The policeman

## MURDER ON THE LYTTON FERRY

could clearly see that both of the Native men who operated the ferry were lying on the deck and they appeared to be unconscious or dead. There were no vehicles on the deck and no sign of any persons other than the two men lying on the deck.

The little river ferry was the type known as a reaction ferry. It was carried back and forth across the river by the current of the water. It was attached to an overhead cable that crossed the river about ten metres above the water level and slightly upstream from where the ferry travelled. A steel frame was attached to the cable and this device could roll along the cable on steel wheels designed and shaped so that their concave surfaces fit closely over the main cable. Sections of additional cable were attached to each end of this device and to each end of the ferry. The ferry operators could change the length of the cables so the ferry would lie at an angle to the river current. Whichever end of the ferry was pulled highest into the current would cause the ferry to move in that direction. The river ferry at Lytton was able to carry only two passenger cars on each crossing or one larger truck or bus.

The relief crew for the ferry was immediately contacted and a small boat was obtained so the police could get out into the river and get aboard the stranded ferry. These arrangements took about another two hours until the first policeman and a man from the replacement ferry crew were able to get onto the deck of the ferry. The first close look at the two men on the deck clearly showed that they were dead and they had died very suddenly and violently. Both men had obviously been killed by a bullet or bullets from a high-powered rifle. The investigating officer was quite sure that the shots had been fired from the river shore and everything about the scene indicated that the shooter had been on the Lytton side of the river at the time of the killing. The limited police resources at Lytton were all called into emergency duty. Calls were made for experienced crime scene investigators and crime scene identification experts who would have to come from Kamloops about one hundred and sixty kilometres away.

Photographs were taken of the ferry where it had been stopped and of the river landing on both sides. The secondary crew then moved the ferry into the landing on the Lytton side and tied it there. The bodies were covered and preliminary examination of the ferry deck was carried out while the police waited for the specialists to arrive from Kamloops. Precautions were taken to keep any unauthorized persons away from the scene.

Two policemen began searching the area where the shots were suspected to have been fired from. The ground was entirely made up of rock and gravel but after some time two expended rifle cartridges were located and it seemed that this showed the location of the person or persons who had fired the fatal shots. It appeared that the shots had been fired from behind a rock which lay just above the high water mark of the river. Marks in the

## MURDER ON THE LYTTON FERRY

gravel and several fresh cigarette butts indicated that some person had lingered there for some time before or after the shots had been fired.

Word of the murder spread rapidly around the community and the Native reserve. Within a short time the police had been advised that a sixteen-year-old Native youth had been seen by some of his neighbors earlier in the day. At the times of the sightings he was in possession of a hunting rifle equipped with a telescopic sight. The youth was well known in the small community; he was the victim of severe fetal alcohol syndrome and was therefore not able or willing to comply with many of the responsibilities normally expected of someone of his age. The tragedy was added to by the fact that none of the persons who had seen him in possession of the rifle had seen fit to challenge him about the gun or to report this potentially lethal situation to the police.

Investigators immediately attended at the home of the suspected youth. His mother did not know where he was and she had not seen him since the evening before when he left home for an unknown destination. This was not an unusual situation among the local Natives. There are Native reserve lands on both sides of the Fraser River at Lytton and there are other reserves in several locations within walking distance of Lytton. Young people and any other persons from these reserves frequently stayed with friends and relatives at a variety of places.

49

# WHEN GRAMPA WAS A MOUNTIE

Parental supervision for persons the age of the suspect was very minimal.

The investigational specialists began to arrive and the grisly scene was thoroughly examined. The bodies were removed and preparations were underway to get the ferry back into service.

All available police were working to locate the suspect youth. Many uniformed police were coming and going from the Lytton office as they scrambled to locate and remove the obvious danger of this suspect from the community. All attempts at locating the suspect had come up empty. In spite of the suspected youth being well known in the little community among both the Native and non-Native populations no one we interviewed could recall having seen him since the time of the shootings.

Late that same afternoon a lone policeman was seated by the radio in the Lytton office when he was startled by the sudden appearance of a Native youth at the front counter. The young man had barged in through the office door and laid a telescopic sight equipped rifle on the counter. The startled policeman sprang to his feet and lunged to the counter to get his hands on the firearm. He grabbed the rifle and placed it on the floor out of the reach of the youth on the other side of the counter. Before the policeman could start any conversation, the youth stated, "I killed those guys on the ferry."

The crisis was over; but the shock and horror of the day

## MURDER ON THE LYTTON FERRY

was still developing as more citizens became aware of what had happened.

The young man was arrested and placed in a cell in the office lock-up. The investigation continued and the young suspect was interviewed in detail. He seemed to have no specific motive for shooting the two ferry operators; it seemed he was walking around with the rifle that he had borrowed (without permission) from one of his neighbours, when he happened onto a location near the ferry landing. He was partly concealed by a large rock he used to steady the rifle as he looked at the two men through the telescopic sight. The next thing he knew he had fired two or more shots and both men were laying dead on the ferry deck.

Questions were asked of the suspect about what he had been doing in the time between the ferry incident and his coming into the police office. His answer raised the hair on the back of many police necks.

After the shooting he had walked along the road from the ferry landing and into the community of Lytton. He had crossed the Thompson River highway bridge and then walked through part of the residential area of his home reserve. He had carried the rifle with him while he made this trek. He made his way up the hillside to the railway tracks that ran directly above and behind the RCMP office. He partly concealed himself in some shrubbery where he was able to see anyone coming and going from the police office almost directly below his location. He had loaded the rifle chamber and the weapon was closed and ready to fire. He then looked through the telescope sight at each policeman who came and left the office. He was watching for a specific member of the Lytton detachment who he knew well and held a deep hatred for. That policeman was very fortunate in that he was on his day off and was out of town. Had he been in the community he would certainly have been called in to the crisis situation and he would almost certainly have been the third victim of the shooter.

The youth was dealt with by the courts over the following months and was found to be mentally unfit to stand trial. He was sentenced to be held in custody for the protection of society. No doubt he will have been free and among society again for many years since that incident.

# Fraser Canyon Avalanche

**During the three years** we lived and worked in Lytton we enjoyed getting away for the three-hour drive to the Vancouver area to visit friends and to do some shopping (mainly groceries). We tried to make one of these little excursions about once every sixty days. Whenever we talked among the other police families in Lytton we called the trips to the coast, "an opportunity to see the big lights and to blow off some accumulated stink." Such adventures soon became a traditional thing for those of us stationed there.

Pat and I loaded our little car with all the things we needed along with our two kids and away we went during the last week of January. The trip was a good one on the way there and during the full day and part of the next day that we were able to stay. The roads were clear and dry on our way to the Coast but a weather system had crossed the lower part of the province during the first night that we were there. Rain fell as only it can in the Vancouver area where we were staying with friends. We were more than a little concerned that the storm would be dumping snow wherever it passed outside of the coastal area and our fears soon were realized. The weather reports confirmed considerable snow had fallen over the southern interior of BC.

The return trip was going very well until we reached Hope and learned the storm system had dumped a particularly heavy snowfall in the Fraser Canyon. The Trans-Canada Highway was closed because of several relatively small snow sloughs between Hope and Lytton. The road closure was expected to be in effect for as long as forty-eight hours. Without this rude interruption we would have stopped for our evening meal at the Lake of the Woods restaurant just north of Hope and then arrived home in time to have the kids in bed by about 8:00 p.m.

That was obviously not going to happen on this trip. To complicate matters, I was scheduled to give evidence at a trial in Lytton the next morning. During those times there were no excuses for a policeman to not be available for a scheduled trial so we were very aware that I was in dark brown trouble.

We sought out a well-known truck stop in Hope and decided we would have supper there. During supper we talked to some of the truck drivers about the possibility of taking the three hundred

## FRASER CANYON AVALANCHE

and twenty-five kilometres of secondary road through Princeton, Merritt and Spences Bridge and finally into Lytton. There were some drivers there who had just come into Hope from Princeton; they advised that section of the road was in fairly good winter condition with some snow covering and limited visibility in a few places due to fog. There were no drivers who had been on the road to Merritt which was not surprising as the Coquihalla Highway was still many years in the future and all truck traffic in those years used either the Hope, Princeton and South Okanagan route or the Fraser Canyon through Lytton.

Traffic was often delayed through the Fraser Canyon by rockslides and snow avalanches, big and small.

# WHEN GRAMPA WAS A MOUNTIE

The land rises abruptly from Princeton toward Merritt and then drops again toward Spences Bridge. I was aware of this but decided that I would keep it to myself and we would attempt the drive. I fueled up the car while Pat prepared a little nest in our back seat for each of our kids and away we went. Fortunately we had good winter tires on our little Volvo, and four very winter road weary people arrived in Lytton just before three o'clock in the morning.

I showed up for work at eight that same morning and was prepared to present my evidence in the scheduled trial which was to begin at ten. It was about nine-thirty when we were notified that the circuit judge and the defence lawyer had held a little conference in Kamloops and decided the matter must be set over for a more suitable time when travel was less hazardous.

Short nights have never had a very positive effect on my attitude and this news caused me to mutter, "Oh darn!" or words to that effect.

# Alberni Tsunami

**During my years in** the RCMP it seemed that every incident, regardless of how insignificant, was unfailingly put to paper. The result of this policy requirement left us with a continuous backlog of paperwork but the logic of it all became more obvious as the years went by.

I was therefore quite surprised to find that some very significant actions by several RCMP members during the tidal wave (tsunami) that struck Port Alberni are not recorded for the general information of all Canadians. The tsunami hit the Alberni Inlet following a large earthquake in the Aleutian Islands of Alaska on Good Friday, March 28, 1964. The RCMP played a very large role during the tsunami and the required security of all the millions of dollars of goods and property that was laid waste by it. This story deals mainly with the work done by two RCMP members at the outset of the tsunami and in the days and weeks following. Many

# WHEN GRAMPA WAS A MOUNTIE

RCMP members were involved before the incident was over but there are simply too many to detail here.

Port Alberni lies at the end of a long fjord-like channel stretching inland from the open Pacific toward the centre of Vancouver Island. The actual tsunami wave on the open ocean was not of a great significance but the funnel shape of the Alberni Inlet caused the water to rise to much greater heights at the inland end. The inlet is 25 or more kilometres wide at the ocean and it then narrows quite suddenly about 20 kilometres from the open Pacific to a width of about five kilometres. From that point it tapers continually over the remainder of its length of about 45 kilometres to the Port Alberni Harbour. This geographical oddity caused the tidal wave to become much higher with every kilometre of travel up the inlet. The wave came in two surges: the first rose to about two and one-half metres above the historically established high tide line and spread into the town areas of the two communities of Alberni and Port Alberni. That wave dropped away very quickly but the second came back in a very short time and rose to about nine and one-half metres above the high tide line. The rising water did not come into the inlet as a rushing wall of water as some reports would lead us to believe. It came up more like a very rapid tide that just forgot to stop rising. The speed of the retreating wave was very fast by tide standards; records indicate that the water

# ALBERNI TSUNAMI

in the Alberni Harbour dropped by nine metres in thirty minutes during the ebb.

These two communities of Port Alberni and Alberni lay side by side at the end of the Alberni inlet but each place had their own municipal council and each had a policing contract with the RCMP. Alberni lay to the north and Port Alberni was to the south. The two communities later amalgamated (on October 28, 1967). The name Port Alberni was chosen to identify the combined communities. The police boat *Ganges* was based at Port Alberni detachment but worked for both detachments along with every other police establishment on the west side of Vancouver Island. The bulk of the administration work from the boat was done through the Port Alberni detachment.

One of the key figures of this story is Bernard "Bernie" Mason who was born in Newfoundland on January third 1933 and he joined the RCMP marine division as a marine special constable #M-137 in 1959. He worked on the police boats out of Halifax for one year and then accepted a transfer to work on the police patrol boat stationed at Tofino. His transfer involved about the longest move that is possible from East to West in Canada. Shortly after he arrived in Tofino, Bernie met his wife-to-be who was working as a public health nurse among the Native Indians on the west coast of Vancouver Island. The two were married and over the next years they worked at several locations on the British Columbia coast.

# WHEN GRAMPA WAS A MOUNTIE

In 1965 Bernie converted to a regular member of the RCMP however he continued working on the police boats. He had by then obtained his *Certificate of Marine Competency* through additional courses and training. In 1975 the Mason family was transferred to Newfoundland where they lived and worked for two and one half years; Bernie was promoted to sergeant on his move to Newfoundland. Their next move took them back to the British Columbia coast at Prince Rupert where he was promoted to Staff Sergeant. Shortly after their arrival in Prince Rupert, Bernie left the marine section and worked as a regular land-based policeman. In 1982 they transferred to Courtenay on Vancouver Island and remained there until Bernie retired to pension in 1988. Bernie and his wife still live in the Comox Valley on Vancouver Island.

The other member was Sergeant Stanley B. "Stan" Green, RCMP #19794, who was in charge of the police boat *Ganges* at that time. Stan had spent most all of his adult life at sea starting as a deck hand and continually improving his deep sea qualifications until he had become one of the most qualified mariners on the entire Canadian West Coast. He had qualified himself for an *International Deep Water Mate Certificate* when he was only twenty-four years old. Stan had changed from deep water to coastal vessels on the British Columbia coast and he then applied to the RCMP where his extensive qualifications immediately put him in charge of one of the coastal police boats. Stan was in his mid-forties at the time of the tsunami in 1964. Stan had seen tidal waves during his life at sea and one of these had been a very major event. Fortunately for the people of the Alberni Inlet, he applied his past knowledge and skills to the situation they all faced that night; without Stan's help the damage would have been much greater. Stan died after many years of retirement at Comox on September 27, 2003.

Equipment and knowledge in the marine areas of the world have come a long way since those times. Earthquakes are immediately detected by instruments which monitor seismic events and the information is broadcasted to the world within minutes of the occurrence. Warnings are immediately spread to all places at risk of a tsunami and people can begin to take precautionary actions such as getting their families to higher ground and preparing their boats to withstand such an occurrence. None of these technical services were available in 1964.

Stan and Bernie were enjoying a few days of time on land with their families on the night of the tsunami. That evening Bernie had intended to take in the television news and then enjoy a good sleep without the constant motion of his home away from home on the *Ganges*. The news made him aware that a large earthquake had struck in the Aleutian Islands and there was a definite possibility of tsunami waves all along the west coast of North America. He immediately contacted his sergeant by telephone and made him aware of what he had heard. He then drove his car to the wharf nearest where the *Ganges* was tied; they had agreed to meet there and survey the situation. It was about 11:30 p.m. when he arrived to immediately see that the water was way above the high-tide mark and it was still rising rapidly. He parked his car and met with Stan near the large wharf where two ocean-going ships were tied while they loaded lumber from the local mills. The crew on these boats had become aware of the wave and they had adjusted the ties that secured the boats to allow them to float much higher than they normally would. Bernie and Stan immediately saw that a third ocean-going ship that had been tied at another large wharf to load material from the pulp mill had broken loose at the stern and was in extreme danger. The stern of the ship had swung inland on the rising water and was completely reversed from the proper position it should have occupied. Stan and Bernie immediately sprang into action; Stan set about getting aboard the loose ship while Bernie drove to the closest police office to make them aware of what was happening and suggest that the afternoon shift be kept on duty to help with the crisis they were facing.

Marine law and insurance concerns demand that an ocean-going ship must not be moved once it is tied in a harbour unless there is a qualified harbour pilot on board. Sergeant Green was very aware of all these regulations and when he got on board the ship he found that the only people on board were deck hands who

## ALBERNI TSUNAMI

spoke very little or no English. All the ship's officers and senior staff had left the ship and gone to Vancouver to enjoy some shore time while the loading was done. With his extensive experience and marine qualifications he chose to take matters into his hands and attempt to save the ship. Stan knew from his previous tsunami experience that when the water receded the entire upper end of the inlet would be drained dry. The position of the reversed ship would leave the stern high on the rocky shore while the stem would fall into the void left by the receding water. He was certain that the ship would break its back if this was allowed to happen. He took command of the ship and with the help of the crew and a tug boat he moved it back to the normal position alongside the wharf where it was re-tied so that, with constant adjustments to the lines, it too could survive the receding water.

When Bernie got back from the police office he found there was about two metres of water where he had parked his car only a short time before. Soon the first surge had reached its crest and receded, but the second and much larger surge was soon well under way.

They moved and retied the police patrol boat so it would not be swamped by the surging and receding water.

The excess water generated some rather comical situations. A local radio station had their studios on the third floor of the Barclay Hotel which was well within the flood area. The radio

WHEN GRAMPA WAS A MOUNTIE

host on duty that evening had looked out his window to see water where it had never been before; the water completely surrounded the hotel building he was in and he was quite certain the hotel was about to float away. He could clearly visualize the hotel floating away and rolling over as it went. His cries for help and/or guidance were broadcast to the community and were a source of jokes and pity for a long time after the crisis. The high water mark in the lobby of the hotel was about two metres up the walls of the building which was a long way short of floating it away but the fellow on the radio had no way of knowing that; and he had no way of knowing when or if it would ever stop.

When Bernie and Stan were making their way to the police boat in a dingy, they passed by a little boat that had been the home of a local man for several years. This man had an alcohol problem which was largely responsible for him having to live on the small boat. As the two policemen neared the boat they could hear the frantic screams of the fellow as he stood at the stern of the boat and looked down at the lights of the town which had always been well above his line of vision. The sight of these lights below his boat had totally un-nerved him and he was making this fact very obvious.

Stan and Bernie worked continuously over the following days, very involved in the prevention of looting and in advising other policemen on problem areas they observed as they went

## ALBERNI TSUNAMI

about the area. Bernie left home just after eleven p.m. on Friday and he finally got home for a change of clothes on Tuesday afternoon. Stan had very likely done about the same hours but we have no record of it. The day after the flood, the RCMP brought in an additional twenty-five policemen from around the island and the lower mainland area.

The additional police maintained 24-hour security on a huge triangle of the two municipalities where the greatest damage had occurred. This security coverage was maintained around the clock for twenty-one days until the many insurance adjusters and the Canadian Army Corp of Engineers began to assess and clean-up the damage.

The damage was in excess of ten million dollars; and that was in 1964 dollars. As soon as an area had been documented in detail by the insurance adjusters, the Army people moved in with bulldozers to pile and burn the destroyed homes and business places.

The tidal pattern of the entire Alberni Inlet was abnormal for the rest of that summer. Fishermen and all marine traffic were left with a bit of a guessing game if they were required to go into any areas around the inlet. Bundles of lumber were floating all over the area and several local people made some extra money by salvaging and securing these valuable things. Many bundles broke apart as they drifted around the inlet leaving areas that looked almost like a person could walk across on the floating lumber.

## WHEN GRAMPA WAS A MOUNTIE

The tsunami caused damage at many locations along the open ocean side of Vancouver Island. A Native Indian community at Hot Springs Cove lost many homes to the sudden surge of water. A logging camp at Fair Harbour was also damaged extensively. These two locations were located where the water was funneled in by a cove or inlet and they received a similar high water effect as Port Alberni though to a much lesser degree. Minor flood damage happened at many other locations along the BC Coast in that same event.

The actions by these two policemen were very significant in reducing some of the flood damage that night; their combined actions saved an unknown number of boats all the way from the ocean-going ship that had broken loose to small dinghies that would have been carried away by the high water. The prior knowledge of tsunamis by Sergeant Stan Green and the assistance provided by Bernie Mason were very beneficial to the other policemen who were called on to deal with all the emergencies the people of the area were exposed to. Even the drunken fellow on the little boat and the radio announcer received some reassurance from these two that will have helped them to cope with a great unknown.

# Coffee Creek Bluffs

**During mid-summer of 1964,** the family of a Nelson businessman came to the office to report that he had not been seen or heard from for several days. His car was also missing so it was assumed he had driven away or had been involved in some mishap on any of the mountain roads around the district. He was a well known man in the Nelson business community and everyone we spoke with was surprised to hear he was missing. This type of disappearance was definitely not something he had been inclined to do.

The family and business associates told us he had been struggling with a drinking problem but had most often been able to confine this demon to his non-working times. All the usual inquiries came up empty; the lady who was his office assistant advised that she had been worried about him because of his recent mood

## WHEN GRAMPA WAS A MOUNTIE

swings and the increasing tendency to have the smell of liquor on his breath when he was working and meeting with people.

The vehicle description and that of the missing man were distributed to the police offices in the Kootenay region but no information came to light over the following few days. The local paper featured a missing man story about him and the next day a local citizen came to our office to tell us he was quite sure he had seen the man and his car near a location known as the Coffee Creek Bluffs along the main body of Kootenay Lake. The sighting was in the mid-afternoon of the day the man was last seen by his family and associates; he was reported to have been sitting in his stationary vehicle near the north end of the bluffs. The Coffee Creek Bluffs lie to the east and north of Nelson by about forty kilometres.

A few hours later two men who had been fishing at Queens Bay came to our office with a very heavy, water-logged briefcase they had found floating in the lake. The area where they had been fishing is in the current path of the lake which flows from the area of the Coffee Creek bluffs into the West Arm of the lake and then toward Nelson. The briefcase and the contents were soon positively identified as belonging to the missing man and his business.

The bluffs are the location of one of the longest electrical powerline spans in the world. The power line carries electrical energy from the Kootenay River hydro dams near Nelson to the

## COFFEE CREEK BLUFFS

industrial and residential customers in the East Kootenay region of British Columbia. This site was chosen for the line crossing because of the extremely high cliffs that rise from the lake shore to about one thousand feet up where the power lines begin their span. The roadway which runs along the west shore of the main body of Kootenay Lake lies about four hundred feet above the lake water where enough rock could be drilled and blasted away to allow for a minimal width of roadway. This roadway was a scary place for anyone to linger and it was extremely so for anyone with an aversion to heights.

An immediate patrol was made to the bluffs. The road surface across the bluffs consisted of very well compacted earth and gravel. There were concrete barricades along the outer edge of some parts of the one-half kilometre section of cliff-side roadway but there were many gaps where the roadway was just too narrow to allow traffic and also have room for these safety devices. Near the center of the bluff section we found faint marks where it appeared a vehicle had made a very sudden acceleration from a point close to the wall on the inside of the roadway. The track of a spinning wheel made an arc across the narrow roadway and through an opening between the concrete barriers and then into the open air. My partner and I took turns leaning out over the edge of the roadway to try to see as much of the bluffs below as possible but we were not able to see any indication of an impact from

69

a vehicle or any pieces of it. We did see what we were quite sure was the rainbow colors of an oil slick on the water directly below where the tire marks had left the roadway. Part of the missing man mystery appeared to be solved.

The day was about used up by that time so the investigation was set over to the next morning when we towed the RCMP's trailer-mounted sixteen-foot boat and its forty horsepower outboard to the boat launching facility nearest the Coffee Creek Bluffs. It was a beautiful summer day and we both agreed that we would have much preferred if our early morning start had been for

View across Kootenay Lake from Coffee Creek Bluffs.

## COFFEE CREEK BLUFFS

the purpose of trying to catch some of the monster rainbow trout Kootenay Lake was famous for.

We fired up the outboard and made our way along the shoreline until we reached the foot of the Coffee Creek Bluffs. At first there seemed to be nothing to be found there but we again saw a thin sheen of an oil slick on the lake surface. Closer examination showed that droplets of oil were rising to the surface and then dispersing slowly over the water. The oil particles were quite thick because of the coldness of the lake water. We scooped up several of these just as they reached the surface and concluded that they were motor oil.

The lake survey records we had accessed indicated that there was two hundred to two hundred and fifty feet of water at the base of the bluffs and that the cliff continued steeply into the lake for most of that depth. The oil droplets were surfacing about twenty metres from where the water met the cliff so we assumed there was only a slight outward slope on the cliff below the water line.

Back at our office we discussed what we had learned and arrangements were made for a local scuba diver to meet with us and discuss the situation. The diver was a local fellow who had assisted us on a variety of underwater happenings over the recent past. He was totally fearless, or so it seemed, and there was some discussion about allowing this fellow to attempt such a deep dive. He assured us he had done similar dives on a number of occasions

WHEN GRAMPA WAS A MOUNTIE

and did not see this location as any more dangerous than others. We set up our plans to return to the site early the following day.

The next morning we were back at the boat launch site before breakfast with our volunteer scuba diver and all his gear. The weather was suitable to get to the bluffs but there was a wind warning for later in the day and we wanted to get this job done before the wind came up and forced us off the area. My partner and I were very unfamiliar with scuba diving procedures but suggested that we could put a small anchor down once we reached the site so the diver would have a line to follow. He rejected this immediately saying it would likely create more problems and danger than it would solve.

We drove our boat up the lake and soon were on the spot in question. We could still see small oil droplets coming to the surface though there seemed to be slightly longer intervals between them. The diver finished getting into the last of his gear and without another word he rolled backwards over the gunwale of the boat and was gone from sight. The bubbles from his breathing were very obvious for the first few minutes after he left the boat but as he went down the bubbles became less visible and soon there were only very fine bubbles almost like those rising from a nice cold beer. The two of us in the boat were left to "hurry up and wait" for the few minutes that seemed like several days until he again surfaced.

## COFFEE CREEK BLUFFS

The diver came up and advised that he had found a body only about fifty feet below the surface. The body was a man and he was caught by some of his clothing that had become hooked over a jut-out of rock. The diver had also found a bumper from a car and there was a license plate attached to it. This was on a ledge only a few metres above where the body was located. The diver went down again with a line from our boat and he attached it to the body so we could haul it up and into our boat. Another dive with the line brought up the bumper and license plate.

A radio call to our office was made to advise the local coroner we were coming off the lake with a body. The coroner arranged for a funeral home to attend and take possession of the body when we landed.

The three of us and our cold and stiff passenger returned to the boat launch. Our diver put his gear into his vehicle and drove away with only our thanks and appreciation for his great contribution.

As soon as it arrived in Nelson, the body was positively identified by a family member. The license plate was registered to the dead man. Another tragic mystery was solved and the family was left to begin their healing process.

No attempt was ever made to recover the wreck from the depths of the lake. Environmental concerns would most likely not allow for such a casual attitude in the world of today.

# Cougar

**It was during the** Christmas school break on January third that this horrible event happened near the little community of Shaw Springs in the Thompson River valley. Shaw Springs lies near the mid point between Lytton and Spences Bridge. The Thompson River canyon is still quite narrow at Shaw Springs and it is nearly filled by the river, the highway, and the two major railways.

A financially-challenged family had found a home they could afford to rent because of the semi-isolated location. The home was very basic but a long way ahead of what they could afford if they were in a location closer to any large community. The father was the main wage earner with work in the construction industry; his work took him into many locations around western Canada where he frequently had to live in a camp and was often only home every second weekend. With that situation, the home

# COUGAR

location was of much less importance to the young family and they were quite satisfied there.

There were three children; a twelve-year-old boy and his two sisters who were about ten and eight. The children were taken to and from school in Spences Bridge on a short schoolbus ride morning and afternoon.

The Thompson valley had received a generous dump of snow just in time for Christmas and the children were making the most of the school holidays by playing in the thirty centimetres of snow around their home. The three children had planned to make their way downriver, between the highway and the Canadian Pacific railway to a point about two hundred metres from their home. They had taken turns breaking a trail through the snow as they made their way in single file toward a place where a wooden culvert passed under the railway grade. They were a bit curious about this dark passage under the tracks but they did not enter it, mainly because of their fear of the darkness. They played in the snow near the mouth of the culvert for a short time and then they started back toward their home. The three were again in single file with the brother bringing up the rear.

The father was home for the holidays and he and his wife were startled by screams as the two girls ran toward their home. The hysterical children told their mom and dad that a big cat had knocked their brother down and it was biting at his head and arms. The parents knew immediately that this was a cougar attack.

The father grabbed his rifle and ran toward the place indicated by his daughters. The mother ran to a neighbouring home and told the terrifying story. The man from that home immediately grabbed his rifle and ran down the railway tracks toward the culvert crossing area.

The father of the boy had arrived a few minutes before his neighbor appeared on the railway grade above him. He had found the marks in the snow where his son had been knocked down; there was a terrifying amount of blood smeared around the attack area; drag marks and a blood trail led from there into the dark culvert. The father had hesitated about firing his rifle into or through the culvert in the hope that his son was still alive.

Upon the arrival of the neighbour, the father shouted that he was going into the culvert and asked the man to watch the other end. The culvert size forced the man to be on his hands and knees as he entered. Soon after getting into the darkness of the culvert the man's eyes became accustomed to the limited light and he was able to see the silhouette of a cougar where it was crouched near the middle of the culvert. He levered a cartridge into the chamber of his rifle and fired a shot at the cougar while trying to stay as high on the animal as he could place the shot because he knew it was crouched over his son.

# COUGAR

The cougar howled a frightening sound as it bolted along the culvert away from the man with the gun. The neighbor on the railway grade saw the cougar as it burst out of the culvert in full flight. He fired two shots at it before it reached the cover of some scrub pine trees, thinking he had hit it with the second shot but he was not sure. He ran along the railway tracks trying to get another sighting of the animal but it seemed to have disappeared into thicker tree cover further up the hillside.

The neighbor ran back and down the side of the railway grade to the point where the father had entered the culvert. As he reached the opening he could hear the sobs of the father as he struggled out of the dark hole with the obviously dead body of his son in his arms.

The frantic mother had called the police office in Spences Bridge and told her tragic story to the constable there. I was patrolling the highway near Lytton when I heard the radio message and drove toward the scene as quickly as the road conditions allowed. I met the Spences Bridge policeman near the culvert where I learned that an ambulance from Ashcroft had attended and removed the child's body in preparation for the coroner's investigation.

We followed the tracks of the cougar in the snow to where we could plainly see that a bullet had struck the animal as it tried to escape. The neighbour had demonstrated some skilled shooting by hitting the racing cat. The animal was lying dead just into the edge of the bush cover. We dragged the carcass out to the highway, wrapped it in a tarpaulin and put it into the Spences Bridge police car.

The forensic examination of the dead cat indicated that it was about twelve years old; it was a male nearly eight feet in length and it weighed just under ninety pounds. The animal was emaciated but there was no obvious reason for this condition except its age. There were abundant deer and other smaller prey animals in the area. The conservation office officials concluded that the cougar must have been somewhat feeble due to age and it had attacked the child by instinct and in desperation. We were unable to find any cougar tracks in the snow around the area; this indicated that the cat had been "holed up" in the railway culvert for several days before the attack.

The cause and logic applied to this investigation did little or nothing for the grieving family of the dead child.

# Anahim Lake Patrol

**During the years we** were stationed at Williams Lake, I was working highway patrol. This duty allowed a certain amount of freedom from the routine tending to local town complaints from the public but there were frequent calls to attend all but the most minor traffic accidents. My work often extended into the wee hours of the night but in the overall it was a most interesting and challenging job.

There were, of course, some more advantages to my patrol job; we were never scheduled to work from midnight until eight in the morning and if we were out during those times, there was usually a good reason and the situation was interesting enough to make the time go by very quickly. In such incidents we just operated with a little less sleep the following day and hopefully we were early to bed the next evening. Those of us scheduled to work from five to seven nights in a row were faced with the

# WHEN GRAMPA WAS A MOUNTIE

necessity of sleeping during the day. Day sleeping was something I always found difficult and it would have been much more so during our Williams Lake years because we had two pre-school-aged children.

Another of the positive aspects of working there was the fact that Williams Lake lies at the eastern end of BC Highway 20. Highway 20 crosses the Chilcotin Plateau between Bella Coola on Pacific tidewater, and Williams Lake on the high interior plateau. The rugged Chilcotin area has always been one of my favorite parts of the province. Whenever possible during the summer, my partner and I would arrange an extended patrol into the depths of the Chilcotin where we would deal with the numerous logging trucks that hauled wood from that area to feed the huge appetites of several large mills in Williams Lake. Many of these trucks were in a state of disrepair due to the tough road conditions and the belief among many of the drivers that they could get away with a few minor defects like brakes and lights because – after all – this was the Chilcotin. The dirt roads of the Chilcotin tended to support some of the log truck drivers arguments. They felt that lights on the rear end of a truck, in a cloud of dust like these machines generated, were of little value so they were frequently in need of repair. We tried to be reasonable with these men who were working under some extreme conditions, so we certainly did now *"write 'em up"* for the first minor defect.

## ANAHIM LAKE PATROL

The dusty roads of the Chilcotin were legendary. After one of these patrols I could actually feel the additional weight in my uniform trousers from the saturation of dust particles. The police cars were so full of dust that our service man told us he had to dump his vacuum cleaner several times before the car was done. My wife clearly recalls my homecomings from these patrols with my teeth and eyeballs the only clean appearing parts of me.

Now I think that the foregoing is about sufficient justification

Our patrol car beside our lakeside accommodations. We'd find a place that would provide a boat and motor with the unit. The rainbows were waiting!

for our Chilcotin patrols. However, to us, the main reason for these trips was the fact that many of the little lakes in that area were teaming with beautiful pan-sized rainbow trout. In spite of the clear call of duty, we would sometimes (okay, frequently) shut down the police activity fairly early in the afternoon to allow a little time on the water during the long summer evenings. We soon learned which of the few motels in the region provided a small lake boat and motor as part of their room package and our business was directed exclusively to these establishments.

The operators of these carefully selected motels soon learned that we were fairly regular customers and that their food freezer units were very useful for the preparation of our fish for the long haul back to Williams Lake. These considerations made for a very restful and productive patrol with only the logging truck drivers being glad to see us go.

After one of the Chilcotin patrols I took my twenty-four little rainbows to a specialty butcher shop in Williams Lake where the owner-operator cured and smoked them to perfection. The call came that my fish were ready on the same day that it happened to be my turn to host our regular poker night. This poker night had been a long-time tradition at Williams Lake. The whole available police establishment along with our cell guards would gather for a game at a different home of one of the cops about every sixth week of the year. The contest was limited to ten cent maximum

## ANAHIM LAKE PATROL

bets and not more than three raises. An unskilled, honest-faced poker player like myself was very seldom a winner but a bad loss night would only amount to about five dollars. My biggest poker loss of the two-and-one-half years in Williams Lake happened the night that I mistakenly offered a taste of my fresh smoked Chilcotin rainbows. Before the last card was dealt the last tiny fragment of my beautiful fish was gone; the bastards ate it all.

# Archie and
# the Six-Toed Dog

**This story comes out** of the Central Cariboo town of Williams Lake in about the middle of the 1960s. I was privileged to serve there around that time and I still consider it a stroke of luck that I was selected for duty there.

Williams Lake was a rough and tumble place that was inhabited by a great variety of people. Many, including of course the Native population, had lived there for generations and they were all totally infatuated with the place. This was somewhat unique in the central part of the province. It seemed to me many communities were inhabited in large part by people who had come there only because there were a variety of good jobs available; most of those people harbored thoughts about leaving after the next payday. Sadly, many of those folks spent their life with such depressing thoughts but their eventual departure frequently involved a

## ARCHIE AND THE SIX-TOED DOG

layer of Cariboo sod. This is not to say that there were not some truly great citizens in all communities; only that Williams Lake felt like it had an over-abundance of fine folks. I could sense the Williams Lake people liked their surroundings; their general attitude clearly displayed this mind-set. The smaller communities and ranches surrounding Williams Lake all benefited from this positive spin; the result was a great assortment of odd local characters and truly good people. Very often the odd character and the truly good person were one in the same.

The life of a cop was not an easy one in Williams Lake but the overall experience was always interesting and exciting after the bruises had healed and a few scores had been squared away. Even the local roustabouts seemed to have a bit of the positive community spin; it seemed that each one of them were intent on building their local reputation by physically putting down one of the local cops, yet they harboured no resentment if their attempt fell short, or in some cases way short. The odds were actually in favor of the cop because his opposition had most often spent too much time bolstering his courage with booze. Assault charges against the police were few and far between; the next meeting with one of these challengers usually involved a hand shake and an apology. Each duty shift brought something new and interesting or so it seemed, partly because the community's positive spin spread quickly to us and our overall attitude.

# WHEN GRAMPA WAS A MOUNTIE

It was after midnight when a couple of the cops had brought some clients to the lock-up on the second floor of the old Post Office building and they paused to catch their breath and a sip of coffee before hitting the streets again. Their coffee was interrupted by a phone call; one of the aforementioned "good persons / odd characters" was on the line to report that someone had stolen his car. He went on to say that he parked it behind the Lakeview bar during the late afternoon and had left the keys in the ignition as most folks did in those times. He further advised that his black Labrador dog was in the car and he seemed to be more concerned about the dog than the car. The car was a two-tone green 1953 Dodge and the man had owned it since it was new.

The policeman who took the call immediately detected that the complainant had a snoot-full and he questioned him about this. The cop suggested that he may have simply forgotten where he had parked his car and that it would not be a totally bad thing if he was unable to find it until the next morning at the earliest. The caller agreed that he had a bit of a load on but insisted he knew exactly where he parked and that he had been out to the car a couple times during the evening to visit with and to exercise his dog. The information was recorded and then broadcasted by police radio to Quesnel and One Hundred Mile House, and the two men on the following shift in Williams Lake were made aware of the incident. Nothing further came

## ARCHIE AND THE SIX-TOED DOG

to police attention about the car and the dog during the rest of that night.

The cop who had taken the call from the vehicle owner had been called as a witness in a trial at One Hundred Mile House the next morning. After a few short hours of sleep he was again in a police car for the drive to attend Court as required. He drove south on the Cariboo Highway until he stopped to fuel up the police car. He pulled into a service station in Lac La Hache where a man came out immediately to assist with the fuel requirements. The policeman asked this fellow if he had been working late the previous night and the man replied that he had been working. The reason he was doing that was because he was the owner of the business, not at all an uncommon situation in those times.

The policeman asked if he had any recall of a two-tone 1953 Dodge car stopping there in the late evening? The service station man replied that he had been fairly busy until he closed around 2:00 a.m. but he did not recall such a vehicle. Further conversation brought up the fact that there may have been a dog in the car. This information immediately triggered his recall of the vehicle. He had seen the very friendly dog and played with it for a moment through the partly open back window of the car while he pumped five dollars worth of fuel into the tank. The service station man could not recall anything about the person in the car but he was quite certain the driver had been a man and that he was alone.

87

# WHEN GRAMPA WAS A MOUNTIE

The service station man had also noticed a very unusual thing about the dog. It had six toes on each of the front feet. The policeman was a little baffled about this information and reluctantly admitted he was not entirely positive just how many toes a dog would normally have. He did however make a note of this information and that the service station man described the dog as a very nice black Labrador. A radio message back to the Williams Lake police office requested that the car and dog owner be contacted and questioned about the dog's feet. The call confirmed that the dog did in fact have some very unusual front feet. There was no doubt now that this had been the stolen car from Williams Lake.

The car description and details were added to the stolen car bulletins around the province but nothing came in about it over the next week. Shortly into the following week a rancher from the Alkali Lake area reported to the police that he had seen a two-tone green car around his home area on a couple occasions in recent days. Alkali Lake was a mainly rural district with cattle ranches and a large Native reserve. The building site of one of the cattle ranches was right across the road from the reserve and these facilities were considered the centre of the district. The reserve was known among the local police as "Alcohol Lake." The rancher told us that the car had been driven by a Native man and there were several other Natives in the vehicle. Alkali Lake is south and west of Williams Lake but it is still on the east side of the Fraser

## ARCHIE AND THE SIX-TOED DOG

River. A dirt and gravel road then existed and it ran in a fairly direct line from Williams Lake to Alkali Lake but the area could also be accessed by a similar road from the general area of Lac La Hache. The route between Williams Lake and Lac La Hache was a two-lane paved road designated BC Highway 97.

An immediate patrol was made to the Alkali Lake area but their quick search of the district failed to locate the vehicle. The rancher who had seen the car was interviewed and was requested to let the police know if he saw the car again.

The rancher reported another sighting the next day and another patrol was made. The area search again came up empty but there were many places in the local area where a car could be hidden. The two cops were both quite familiar with the local Natives and they held a little conference between them with the goal of selecting the local resident who would most likely have stolen the car. They came to a very quick agreement on the most likely suspect and they attended at this man's home on the reserve. I will call this fellow "Archie" for the purposes of this story. They were met at the door by Archie and they put their suspicions on the line immediately. They described the car and asked him what he could tell them about the disappearance of the car from the Lakeview parking lot. Archie was completely without knowledge of the car. He volunteered that he had not been to Williams Lake in the past month but if he knew anything at all about the car he would

89

immediately tell them. The cops were about to leave but both felt Archie had oversold his innocence although obviously he was not at that moment in the right frame of mind to change his story.

The two policemen were just getting into their car when a beautiful black Labrador dog came bounding over to visit with them. The dog was sleek and glossy and very friendly, a description which definitely did not fit most reserve dogs. It also had six toes on each of its front feet. The jig was up!

When first confronted with the dog evidence, Archie continued to exaggerate his pretended innocence but he soon gave up after learning about the very unusual feet of his new four-legged friend. Archie then told the true story and guided the cops to a little ravine alongside the reserve where the car was partially concealed. Archie was arrested and he got to ride back to Williams Lake in the back of the police car with his six-toed friend.

Archie was charged with theft over two hundred dollars and possession of stolen property over two hundred dollars. The dog and his rightful owner enjoyed a very exuberant reunion and the car owner got a friend to give him a lift to Alkali Lake where he retrieved his car with the keys still in the ignition switch as he had left them about two weeks earlier.

In those times an accused person in these circumstances had the right to choose the method of his trial. The charges were read and Archie was told that he could elect to be tried by a magistrate,

## ARCHIE AND THE SIX-TOED DOG

or by a judge without a jury, or by a judge and jury. Archie was not represented by counsel; he asked to hear the list again and it was repeated. He stated that he had never been before a judge and jury so he chose that method. The case would now have to await the next sitting of the Assize Court. The next opportunity for an Assize trial would be at Quesnel in about six months. Archie was released on bail following a brief preliminary hearing in Williams Lake. He appeared in Quesnel as he had promised to do. The police witnesses were there in their dress uniforms along with the car owner and everything was prepared to go ahead. The case was called; Archie was still not represented by counsel. The court official read the charges and again asked Archie how he would plead. Archie stood erect and faced the judge and jury and announced in a loud voice and with only a slightly muffled laugh, "Guilty to both charges."

The Supreme Court judge must have been impressed with Archie's performance because he sentenced him to sixty days concurrent on both charges. No doubt justice was served at its best!

It was about five weeks after the Quesnel Assize that the same two cops who had met the six-toed dog at Alcohol Lake were again out patrolling the highway just south of Williams Lake. They noted a beautiful shiny new Oldsmobile meeting them on the highway. They both immediately recognized the driver; yes, it was Archie!

They executed a "bootleg" turn with the marked police car and Archie immediately pulled to the side of the highway and stopped. Archie laughed loudly as he reassured them again and again that he had borrowed the car from a friend in One Hundred Mile House. He was just going to Williams Lake to attend to an appointment and then right back to One Hundred Mile House to return the car. A very minor bit of investigation again showed that Archie was fibbing. The car belonged to a doctor who lived at One Hundred Mile House. Responding to a medical emergency, he had run from his car to attend to a patient, leaving his keys in the switch.

Archie for some reason elected trial by magistrate on this one. The magistrate failed to see much humour in the happening and Archie landed himself a sentence of two years less one day at the regional correctional centre in Kamloops.

# Defence of
# Drunken Drivers

**This story took place** in the beautiful city of Nelson in the West Kootenay region, early in the 1960s. A drunken man had been apprehended by a police officer as he drove his car along a public roadway. The man was very disturbed and very vocal in his assertion that the police had nothing more important to do than harass a fine upstanding citizen such as himself. After all, in those days it was considered a right rather than an offence to be able to drive home after a night of partying with the guys. Today we are gradually getting away from this thought pattern but there are still many among us who feel that the current enforcement efforts are an infringement on the rights of citizens. To these thinkers I wish to say, may you join some police officer when, late at night, they knock on the door of some frantic people to tell them why their son or daughter or grandchild will not be coming home ever again, having become another victim of an alcohol-addicted person in a vehicle. Here again we try to reach a compromise between the rights we all cherish and the responsibility we should all respect. Until our civilization makes some great advances along the lines of care and responsibility toward all our fellow citizens, we will unfortunately have to curtail some of the rights we might all enjoy.

The arresting policeman in this case was relatively new to the job with less than one year of field experience. The routine breathalyzer test had shown a blood alcohol level far beyond routine impairment; it indicated complete intoxication. Nevertheless, the concerned citizen hired the most qualified and aggressive and expensive defence lawyer in the region and the matter was brought to trial. The chosen lawyer was a man with a long and successful record as a defence lawyer; he had beaten the system in an amazing number of cases and was known to enjoy putting young policemen through their paces on the witness stand.

The young constable in this case gave his evidence in a very straightforward manner and his final statement was that he had a considerable amount of experience with impaired and intoxicated driving offences. The defence lawyer was obviously very concerned with this part of the evidence and as soon as the crown prosecutor had finished with the young police witness, the defence

# DEFENCE OF DRUNKEN DRIVERS

lawyer sprang to his feet and demanded to know where the young officer had gained all this experience.

The young cop looked him in the eye and said, "My father is the sergeant in charge of the RCMP detachment at Meadow Lake, Saskatchewan. I was employed as a prisoner guard at the detachment and every year we put through about three hundred cases that were very similar to this one."

The expensive and aggressive lawyer stumbled through a couple other routine questions and sat down. His client was convicted. It seemed that the entire defence plan had involved a vigorous attack on a new and inexperienced policeman.

The Province of British Columbia has made some great advances in recent years in the continuing battle against alcohol-impaired vehicle drivers. BC introduced a law which allows a police officer to suspend the driver's licence of a suspected impaired driver at the roadside where the offence has been observed (and typically confirmed with a breathalyzer device). This course of action by the police does not fully satisfy my harsh attitude about these offences but it certainly does allow the officer to deal with the problem in a few minutes and move on to the next offender. The police "road time" has greatly increased by this action, so many more offenders are dealt with who would otherwise have gone undetected. Another positive aspect is a reduction in the wasted police hours dealing with the court trials of impaired drivers and the frequent disappointment for the police person when charges were dismissed on some technicality. The attitude of the general public has been greatly affected by this law; it has become common to hear people decline a server's offer of another drink with the words, "No, thank you, I am driving."

Tragically, in keeping with the philosophy of "rights for the individual," our lawyer-dominated justice system has entertained lawsuits to declare as unconstitutional the British Columbia roadside licence suspension initiative. At this time it appears that some lawyers are working diligently toward the restoration of the "good old days" when we could all drive home after a night at the bar without the interference of the police. I will watch with interest as this unfolds.

# H.E.A.T.
# at Golden

**This story took place** at Golden, BC during the mountain country spring season. The snow was completely gone in the little community and lawns were starting to turn to that beautiful green only seen during that short season of the year. The deciduous tree buds were swelling and a few had released their new leaves, also displaying that special bright green.

I walked to the office most mornings but the walk was so pleasant that day I did not really feel like rushing in to the heaps of paper that made up most days' work. I procrastinated as long as I could and then went in and had a quick look at my desk. There were copies of every incident that had happened since I left the previous afternoon and lots of notes from the other policemen about a variety of happenings.

This morning had a little twist from the normal routine. Lying

# WHEN GRAMPA WAS A MOUNTIE

on my desk was a strange cylindrical object with what looked like a small rocket motor coming out of one end and a semi-pointed cone nose at the other. The thing was about one hundred millimetres in diameter and it was the color that I called olive-drab, the color common on all things military from jeeps and tanks to Hercules aircraft. I was quite certain when I first saw the thing that it was an explosive device. The small rocket engine showed some damage as though it had dropped or crashed in a backwards position.

There was a note taped to the side of this object from one of the constables who had worked the midnight-to-eight shift that morning. The note said someone had found this thing at the side of the highway and brought it to his attention. Not knowing what it was, he had picked it up and brought it to the police office. I was not sure what it was either but the appearance of the thing made the hair stand up on the back of my neck.

I tried to find some comfort by telling myself that this must be a "dud" round that failed to ignite for some reason or perhaps it was one of those inert practice rounds that the military used for training purposes, but it still made me very nervous and I desperately wanted it to be somewhere else.

The early years of the Rogers Pass Highway had been plagued by frequent avalanches that closed the road for long periods while the snow slides were cleared away. This high mountain highway

# H.E.A.T. AT GOLDEN

was a link in the relatively new Trans-Canada-Highway and the frequent closures were obviously causing some political embarrassment and discomfort in high places. The decision was made to do everything possible to keep the new road open. One of the methods of doing this was to cause the accumulated snow high in the mountains to break loose and slide before it attained sufficient mass to reach the highway. Experienced mountaineers knew that once snow had shifted and slid for any distance in the mountains, it would not move again except when it melted and flowed harmlessly away the next spring.

One suggested method to start these desirable small slides was to drop explosive charges from a helicopter. The small explosions would send shock-waves into the snow pack and cause it to break loose. This was done on an experimental basis and found to be quite efficient except that the helicopters required good visibility and calm weather conditions to do their work and the whole endeavour was quite costly. The military people who were involved with the helicopter experiments suggested that a better option for this work would be a 105mm howitzer field gun. This would be one of those fierce-looking devices we have all seen being towed behind a military vehicle. It rides of two truck tires and the barrel extends at an upward angle like a small log. One of these military field guns was brought out to the Rogers Pass and it was found to be the ideal solution. Once all the firing positions had been marked along the highway and the necessary co-ordinates were recorded, the gun could do its job in any sort of weather. It could even be used at night.

The previous winter I had visited with the small group of military men who were stationed in the Rogers Pass just to the west of Golden. Fortunately my visit coincided with the need for snow stabilization and I was able to observe them in action. I had watched with great interest as the big gun was carefully positioned over the previously determined spots. The gun barrel could then be swiveled to a pre-determined position and fired. I had again watched with great interest as the big gun was loaded, it was here that I had seen the nose cone of the ammunition for the big gun and that is what now caused the hair on the back of my neck to rise.

The military detachment from Rogers Pass had very recently packed their equipment and returned to their home base. Had they still been there I would have called on their skills and knowledge to deal with what was now my problem. I placed a call to the military base at Chilliwack, BC and was soon connected with a person who was familiar with military armaments. I described the thing lying on my desk and told him I could see the letters H.E.A.T. stenciled on it. There was a short pause until I heard the words, "Holly Shit." This additional data did little for my neck hairs but we carried on.

# H.E.A.T. AT GOLDEN

I later learned the ordinance on my desk was in fact a bazooka projectile and that these things had been used in some circumstances in the Rogers Pass. The letters on the thing stood for *"High Explosive Anti-Tank"*. Obviously this one had a faulty detonator; it had been fired into the mountains of Rogers Pass where it failed to ignite. A subsequent snow slide must have carried it to the area of the highway where it was picked up by someone who at first thought it was a really neat souvenir. They brought it to Golden before they had second thoughts about it and then they must have thrown it down beside the highway where it was again found and brought to the attention of the patrolling constable. This or a similar combination of happenings must have brought it to find its way onto my desk.

The man on the phone advised that I should immediately evacuate the area until military personnel could attend and dispose of the shell. We talked further about it and how it had been through so much to get to where it was. I was certainly not comfortable around the thing but I was also fairly certain that it would not be easily detonated at this late time. We invited everyone to leave the office while I volunteered to carry it to our little post garage which was nearby but separate from our office building. There I placed sand bags around it until the military ordinance disposal people could attend. Once this could be done we would all breath a little easier.

# WHEN GRAMPA WAS A MOUNTIE

Later that afternoon military people flew to Golden and the projectile was taken to a gravel pit at the edge of town. A small depression was dug out of the gravel and the thing was laid in the bottom along with some additional explosive material and a remote controlled detonator. The signal was sent to the detonator and a very large blast sent shockwaves to where we were standing about a half of a kilometre away. A cloud of dirt and smoke shot into the air. The small shoveled depression was now a sizeable crater. Had this thing chosen to ignite itself during any of the events that brought it to this gravel pit, there would have been one or more very badly scattered bodies. Some spring days are not only beautiful, but also very lucky!

# Horses, For Better, For Worse, and For Moose Hunting

**The horse was the** most important item of the entire arsenal of the NWMP in the days of Sam Steele and James Walsh. The pivotal role for the horse diminished somewhat over the following eighty-eight years that passed until I became a member of the RCMP but the drill instructors and riding masters made it abundantly clear to all of us lowly recruits that we fell far short of even a mediocre horse in overall importance. A good man will be missed for a while; a good horse was irreplaceable.

It was with this as a background that we learned to deal with these huge and seemingly bad-tempered creatures. The outside of a horse was said to be good for the inside of a man and the training regimen of those days made us all very familiar with the outside of horses.

I had a bit of an advantage over many of my troop mates in

# WHEN GRAMPA WAS A MOUNTIE

that I had grown up on a farm in northern Alberta. I had ridden a spirited horse over the seven kilometres to my one-room country school for several years; I had driven a team of horses pulling a sleigh to haul firewood to the farmyard; and I had spent many long hours on a horse-drawn hay rake. Farm boys from those years were considered ready to contribute to the farming operations by the time they had reached the age of twelve or thirteen years. By that age we began to think of ourselves as men; men controlled their emotions and tears were no longer allowed in places where others could see them and become aware of the weakness they indicated.

One of the hardest memories along with some of the best memories of my farm-boy upbringing, of course, involved horses. Queen and Bob were the team best suited to a novice teamster so the three of us began a relationship that became quite involved as we put in many long hours with the hay rake in the hot sun. This team truly lived up to their reputation; nothing that we encountered in all those hours brought these two to even the verge of a run-away. The tractor with the big hay sweep on the front could come within a few feet of them but they acted like it was not even there. The explosive flight of a family of prairie chickens would startle all three of us but Queen and Bob would take it "like a man" and get right back to the job.

In the times between hay-field jobs in the summer, Queen

## HORSES, FOR BETTER, FOR WORSE,
## AND FOR MOOSE HUNTING

and Bob pastured with the other farm horses in a fenced area alongside the farmyard. I remember another farm task involving our large garden: there was a never-ending need to control weeds or to thin the plants to allow the best to flourish. Whenever time allowed I would carry an assortment of vegetables and lush weeds out of the garden and hand feed them to Queen and Bob who would come trotting to the fence, ears forward, as I approached. They would munch happily at whatever I had to offer but their joy was obvious if I had been able to sneak out a few cucumbers or turnips.

The years passed slowly in those times; I finally reached the ripe age of fifteen when the horse-drawn hay rake was replaced by a tractor-pulled machine. This progress made the horses less needed; the only job still left to them was to pull a sleigh to do odd jobs during the winter when a tractor was difficult and time consuming to start. The years had taken a toll on Queen and Bob too; their beautiful bay coats and shiny black manes and tails had lost some of their luster. Their ribs began to show slightly regardless of their diet of the best feed that was available; this was a sure sign that their teeth were failing. I clearly remember the morning when the breakfast table conversation touched briefly on the fact that the last days for Queen and Bob had arrived. I am sure that this conversation did not stimulate the appetite of anyone at that table but my hot porridge suddenly tasted like poplar sawdust.

## WHEN GRAMPA WAS A MOUNTIE

It was later that same day that I heard the sound of the barn door opening and I saw my older brother Don come through the door leading Queen by a halter shank; in his other hand he carried the old .303 Savage Model 99 rifle. They walked slowly toward the far side of the farm yard and the pig pens. I walked quickly to the outhouse, not for the normal routine purpose; I needed a place to be out of sight. From the outhouse I heard the crack of the rifle and the heavy thump as Queen went down for the last time. The uncontrollable tears did not allow me to venture out for quite some time. The following day was Bob's turn and I heard the same sounds from the same location and with a very similar reaction. Thinking back to those times I have grave doubts that I fooled anyone with my sudden trips to the outhouse.

My horse experience had not made me an expert starting my RCMP training by a long way but I had learned that each one of these creatures has a personality and a disposition. I knew that if a horse was having a bad day and wanted to be left alone, he would press his ears back and give me a look that would have translated into a clear message about "sex and travel" had he been a mean street drunk. The mean drunks on the streets were something that I still had to learn about but my farm upbringing gave me some beneficial basic understanding of horses. We had a routine of things that had to be done with each horse every morning; even if the horse did not wish to participate willingly. We very soon

## HORSES, FOR BETTER, FOR WORSE, AND FOR MOOSE HUNTING

learned to move in and tie the halter shank very short to prevent our big friend from striking out like a snake and leaving a brightly colored bite mark on our ass or far worse on the very tender small of our back, either of which would take a very long time to stop hurting. The training routine of that time required eighty hours of riding experience and about double that time grooming horses and cleaning the stables and the saddlery.

The horses were a little unpredictable; many of us had our feet stepped on by one of these animals and there was not a time during the nine months of training that one or more of us were not displaying a brightly-colored horse bite in the showers. We learned that while the horses may not like any or all of us, they would not knowingly inflict a serious injury to us. As our experience increased we were often the stable duty troop on Saturday morning, a time when there were a large number of horses that needed to be cleaned up and exercised by only a few of us. After the first ten minutes in the stable there was not a dry shirt on any of us. After the cleanup we would take thirty-two horses at a time into the indoor riding school and bare-back ride them around the circumference until they were a little warmed up. Following the horse warm-up, we often engaged in a bare-back-wrestling match between two sixteen man and horse teams. The method and rules of this game were very simple: do whatever you can to pull, drag, knock or push one of the opposing team off their horse.

During any of these events there was never a time when there were not several of us lying on the ground with all the horses and riders milling around above and beside us. I clearly recall many of the horses being pushed sideways by other horses and riders and how they would lean to a near fall or willingly buckle their legs to avoid having to step into the area where a rider was on the ground. The horses loved the action and they all took part with enthusiasm but there was an obvious rule among them about not stepping on a man who was down.

I am still convinced that horses have a fairly well developed sense of humor. They loved to bring their rib cages together with the legs of two riders caught in this huge press but they seemed to know that while this was a little painful it would not result in serious injury as would a horse hoof in the unprotected ribs of a downed rider.

Years later while I was a working cop in Prince George I had the opportunity to join a group of friends from the Edmonton area for a mid-November moose hunt in the mountains near Germansen Landing, BC. Larry Erickson, a friend from my growing-up years around Edmonton, had been living at Germansen Landing for years. He made his living there operating a trap line and a hunting guide business. He still lives up there and still loves the area. Larry had a string of saddle horses and pack horses, and made these available to us for a once-in-a-lifetime hunting experience.

## HORSES, FOR BETTER, FOR WORSE, AND FOR MOOSE HUNTING

On our arrival at Larry's home and base camp, we were each introduced to our selected horse and we spent some time establishing a rapport with our new friend. The original plan was for us to ride into the mountains where the moose were known to "hang out." We were to take a mobile camp with the help of pack horses and we would stay until we had our quota of moose or until we had to return to our homes and work. The weather had refused to co-operate with this plan; there was a sudden cold-snap arriving

Each of us was introduced to his mount on arrival at Germansen Landing. Some of us had more horse experience than others.

# WHEN GRAMPA WAS A MOUNTIE

on the day we drove into Germansen Landing and by the time we had unloaded our vehicles the temperature was twenty degrees below zero. Larry decided that, because of the extreme weather, we would ride into the hunt area in the morning and return to his main camp and living facilities every night.

The first morning we were up and in the saddles before day-light. Larry led the group up a good trail in a creek valley that would take us into the high alpine country. Several kilometres of riding brought us to where the ground leveled out and we could see large open areas all around us on the beautiful rolling alpine region.

One of the members of our group was on his first mountain country experience and he was fascinated by the visions and views of the country as we rode along. His horse was a beautiful bay mare that was spirited but gentle; she stepped along quickly and seemed to enjoy herself. As the trail reached the shoulder of the creek valley it passed by a gnarled old pine tree that had a thick limb just a little above saddle horn height and parallel to the ground, reaching out several metres from the trunk. The little mare stepped out of the tracks of the leading horses and without attracting the attention of her rider she passed under the protruding limb and left her rider hanging over the limb like a rag doll. She made only a few more steps to where she stopped and stood looking back as her rider ungraciously made his way to the

## HORSES, FOR BETTER, FOR WORSE, AND FOR MOOSE HUNTING

ground. That horse did this same trick on three of the five days that we passed by that tree. The first time it happened I was quite sure I could see a glint in her eye and a trace of a smile on her lip but on the last occasion her mirth was so obvious that she could well have been laughing aloud and pounding the ground with one front foot. This is another of the many reasons that I have always liked horses and more support for my belief that they do have a sense of humor.

On the second last day of our hunt I was fortunate to encounter a yearling bull moose which I shot. We field dressed it before returning to our cabins. The last day was mostly taken up

This little mare had a great sense of humour. Hal MacDonald and Terry Krause are sizing her up while she does the same with them.

## WHEN GRAMPA WAS A MOUNTIE

by getting a couple of pack horses into the mountains and bringing out the meat. Each of us in the hunting party got a few roasts to take home and enjoy during the coming winter. We all agreed that the moose was entirely a bonus and we would have been very glad to have taken part in the mountain adventure without it.

# The Flying
# Forest Fire

**The hot summer day** at Lytton was going along as most others had during the late summer of 1970. Our routine late summer weather had provided little or no rain for the past eight weeks or more and everything was tinder dry. The Fraser River canyon acts like a giant chimney during this part of the year as a hot wind flows up the canyon in a northerly direction. Not only is the wind hot and dry, it has tremendous strength – so much so that the large evergreen trees that stand in the full exposure to the wind have limbs that reach out mainly from the downwind side of the trunk. This gives the trees a lopsided appearance that was often questioned by newcomers to the canyon area. Another result of these winds are the small rocks that frequently break loose from high on the canyon walls and bounce over the rocks on their way to the river far below. As we worked at our duty along the highway, we often heard the impacts of these rocks as they bounced down the rocky canyon wall. When we heard one above us we tightened the pucker string and waited the few seconds that had to pass until the sound could be heard from below where we were located. There was a feeling of relief each time the sound came from downhill; we had gotten away with another one.

When these missiles passed by very close we heard a whistling sound as they passed through the air! Vehicles were frequently struck by these, including our police cars, but fortunately most strikes were from quite small stones and the damage was minimal. It was not uncommon for one of us to be flagged down by a motorist who had been struck by a small rock. Quite often these Fraser Canyon gravel victims believed they had been shot at. Being "stoned" had a different meaning among the police in the Fraser Canyon in those days.

It was in the early afternoon of another very hot day when an excited person came to the police office in Lytton to advise that a wild fire was sweeping through the forest at a point about five kilometres south of town. We knew at once that this was a bad situation and only going to get worse as the next few hours passed. My partner and I drove toward the source of the smoke and were into the midst of it in a very short time. From our location on the highway we could see the fire moving very rapidly as

## THE FLYING FOREST FIRE

it was fanned by the Fraser Canyon wind. The extreme heat of the fire would cause evergreen trees in its path to suddenly burst into flames with a roar and a scary display of flames shooting high up to where those flames were again carried by the wind into the next available trees. The speed of the fire was frightening under these conditions but it was also spreading itself downwind in giant steps when burning chunks of tree bark and similar material were carried high in the air by the thermal draft of the fire. These smoking and glowing chunks of fuel would then be carried over long distances by the wind to where there would be another sudden outbreak of fire in the tinder-dry brush and trees.

My partner's young wife lived in a home in the town of Lytton and my wife and our two small children were also there. We could see parts of the community from the highway that passed above the town but there was no time to stop in and try to reassure them that they would be evacuated if the situation required that. Our immediate duty was to establish road-blocks on both sides of the fire area to prevent the travelling public from getting into the path of the fire. We picked up another car and established road blocks above the fire in the Thompson River valley and below it in the Fraser Canyon. Shortly after we had the traffic stopped on both sides of the fire area, we received help from the Department of Highways crews from Lytton who brought barricades out and took over manning the road blocks. News of the fire was spread

WHEN GRAMPA WAS A MOUNTIE

to our neighboring police detachments and the Trans-Canada Highway was closed to all traffic at Hope and at Cache Creek; this left us with only the traffic which was already in the affected area to be dealt with locally.

The British Columbia forest service fire crews were on the scene immediately and their leaders put out a call for air tanker support. The nearest air tanker base was at Kamloops, at least an hour of flying time away. We watched for what seemed a very long time until the two old, heavily-loaded World War II Avenger aircraft roared overhead, accompanied by the lighter and faster lead airplane which was known as the "bird-dog". The fire was by then well beyond what the aircraft could deal with. As the aircraft arrived, there was still a group of very dedicated people fighting to save one of the homesteads directly in the path of the fire. This information was either passed to the aircraft by ground radios or it was observed by the crew of the bird-dog. The agile small airplane made two passes over these people and then signaled the bombers to make their strike. Several of the people on the ground were knocked flat by the force of the falling water from the bombers but their job suddenly became manageable and they all were quite sure that the bombers had enabled them to save the home and other buildings.

The fire was above the highway where it had started but it moved very quickly and made many attempts to cross the thin

# THE FLYING FOREST FIRE

barrier of the roadway. All available persons from the area were now patrolling the fire area to try to keep the flames above the highway and therefore away from the bulk of the townsite of Lytton. There were six homes in the direct path of the fire above the highway and to the south of Lytton; four of these homes were lost in the first hours of the fire.

The growth of the community over the years had resulted in the establishment of a little sub-division of the town above the highway. A tremendous effort was put forth by the people from the new area and by many from the old town site and these homes were all saved.

Another scary fact about canyon fires came to light during this fire. The prevailing upstream wind in the Fraser Canyon could actually reverse itself for brief moments as it fought its way up the crooked canyon. This strange wind behavior was very noticeable near the junction of the two major river canyons. Smoke would appear to drop into the river gorge right to the water where it would then rush into the Thompson Canyon or at times it would run south down the Fraser River which was definitely contrary to the prevailing wind direction. It was a frightening sight! These twisting winds could cause a sudden, unexpected and frightening flare up where people were standing shoulder to shoulder to fight the fire.

There was to be little or no sleep for the residents of Lytton

# WHEN GRAMPA WAS A MOUNTIE

that night. Many of the townspeople were out on the fire lines with their garden rakes and shovels in a brave attempt to keep the inferno at bay. The town workmen were gathering any container that would hold some water and they were distributing these water containers along with burlap sacks to the fire lines. A wet burlap sack is very effective to beat down a small grass level fire outbreak and these things saw lots of service over the following hours as every able-bodied man, woman and capable child were pressed into this need.

By early evening the Fraser Canyon winds had subsided somewhat as they nearly always did but there were still a variety of shifting air currents carrying burning embers in a completely unpredictable pattern. The tremendous heat would cause severe updraft winds that would carry embers high in the air to where they sometimes burned themselves out or the air currents would carry them away from the fire and they would then fall back to the ground and start another blaze. These flying embers could easily have carried the fire across both rivers but fortunately this did not happen. Most of us spent the night outside our homes or at vantage points where we could watch for these glowing or flaming missiles and take immediate steps each time one entered the village. No homes were lost within the town and no persons were injured in spite of the huge potential for destruction.

By daylight the next morning the main crisis was past. The

## THE FLYING FOREST FIRE

fire had been stopped or had burned itself out in all but the area well above the village where it continued to climb toward the summit of the mountains to the south and east. Over several days the fire continued toward Lytton Mountain where it finally ran out of fuel and was reduced to a smoldering mass. The water supply for Lytton came from a small creek which had its source near the summit of Lytton Mountain. For the remainder of that summer and well into fall and winter the tap water in the homes of Lytton had a strong smoke smell and there were ashes and partly burned evergreen needles in every glass of water. Apart from the sight and smell in the water I do not recall any adverse effects from it. The folks of Lytton are a tough and hardy bunch.

The following summer the town of Lillooet, about sixty-five kilometres up the Fraser River from Lytton, experienced a similar burn. Many homes around the town were lost in a very sudden and powerful fire that was swept over the area by strong winds. This fire was so strong and fast that there was an immediate move to evacuate mothers and children from the fire path. Several of the families of the RCMP members from Lillooet came to Lytton with little more than the clothes they wore and the family vehicle. Our home in Lytton had a very large recreation room on the lower level and we welcomed the evacuees as best we could. Fourteen people spent the night with us. Fortunately our detachment had just received a new supply of "prisoner mattresses" which consisted

# WHEN GRAMPA WAS A MOUNTIE

of thick foam rubber with a very sturdy plasticized cover. None of these mattresses had seen service in the cells so I went to the office and brought them home for the refugees. The Lillooet fire did not sweep through the town as it appeared destined to do at the outset and our guests were very glad to get the all clear to return to their homes the next morning.

# Fly at
# One Hundred Yards

**This tale has not** a great deal to do with my policing career but it has always been one of my favourites whenever I am among hunters or target shooters. My main hobby over the years in the police business was to do with firearms and hand-loading of ammunition. It was because of this deep interest in ballistics that I earned a little addition to the firearms proficiency badges we wore on the sleeves of our uniform. The badges were crossed rifles and crossed revolvers and required a certain target-shooting score to entitle the policeman to wear them. Those who fired the course and attained the maximum possible score were awarded the right to wear the crossed firearms surmounted by a crown. I displayed the crowns after my fifth year of service until my retirement.

It was a beautiful warm and clear early spring day while I was working from Nelson Detachment. There were still lots of snow patches around in the shaded and higher places but spring was well established. I was patrolling the highway south of Nelson when I noticed that the senior conservation officer was at the rifle range. The shooting range lay alongside the highway a few kilometres out of town. I was not busy with any specific duty at the time so I pulled in to visit with Joe for a few minutes. This man was a firearms expert and he had a wonderful collection of somewhat exotic firearms. It was always interesting to see what sort of firearm Joe was shooting when he was on the range.

Joe had been a member of the British Columbia Provincial Police until 1951 when the provincial policing contract was awarded to the RCMP. Joe had joined the RCMP as the provisions of the contract change had provided, but he soon found the RCMP was not to his liking so he resigned to join the Conservation Officer Service of BC. He seemed comfortable with that choice and he served there until his retirement years later.

I parked and walked over to the shooting bench he was using and we chatted for a few minutes. Joe had a beauty out that day; it was a Swedish-built Sako action with a heavy thick barrel designed for very exacting target shooting. The rifle was mounted with a very powerful telescopic sight more than one half the length of the rifle barrel. The calibre was designated as a .220 Swift and there were not many of those around. The rifle

# FLY AT ONE HUNDRED YARDS

could fire a .22 calibre jacketed bullet in excess of four thousand feet per second and, given very carefully hand loaded ammunition, it did this with amazing accuracy. The goal of people who shot such firearms was to fire a number of shots at a one hundred yard target and have all the bullets go through the same hole in the paper. These rifles were most always rested in sand bags during the shooting because the goal was to test the perfection of the ammunition, the rifle and finally the shooter. Few men were powerful enough to fire such a weapon from the standing unsupported position because the complete gun and scope weighed about thirty pounds.

I set up an extra spotting scope at the shooting bench next to Joe and we peered at the target he was firing at. He told me he had fired three shots but on first glance I had to take his word for it since there was only one hole in the target. Then, on closer examination with the powerful telescope, I could see that the bullet hole was just very slightly out of round. He was preparing to fire another shot as I watched through my scope. The beautiful warm spring day had brought out a large bluebottle fly. This creature was circling lazily around just in front of Joe's target and we could both see it with our telescopes. A moment later the fly landed on the paper target only about an inch from the ragged bullet hole. Joe was steadying up for another shot when I said, "Get that thing!" Joe protested that it would spoil his grouping to which

## WHEN GRAMPA WAS A MOUNTIE

I said, "How many guys have shot a fly at one hundred yards?" Nothing more was said.

Joe shifted the big rifle in the sand bags as I peered at the fly and the target. The rifle cracked and at that instant the fly became a bullet hole in the target. Bits of debris consisting of fly wings and legs scattered to the ground below the target; no doubt the fly "never knew what hit it!" After that day I referred to that rifle in Joe's collection as his "fly rifle."

# The Dirty Thirties
# Escaped Prisoner

**This is a legendary** story oft told within the RCMP. It supposedly really happened, long before I was born.

Many of the "old timers" from my time in the service will occasionally get together and reminisce about the good old days when "men were men" and "a day's work made a day's pay." Those were the times when we were each accountable for whatever we encountered in the line of our duty. We all pine for a return to those times but if we get a little deeper into the subject we can also recall that everything was not "roses" in those times as well. Men from my generation in the Force must struggle with all the changes that have come to pass since our times. No doubt the universe is unfolding as it should; however we do find it difficult to adjust our thinking to get around the new agenda. Perhaps we should give some thought to what the policeman faced in this story and send out a plea for the present generation to "cut a guy a bit of slack." After all, although there can be no valid arguments put forth to show that *all* of our methods required the massive changes that have occurred, there have always been sound reasons to change *some* things.

This old tale comes out of Saskatchewan in the Dirty Thirties. In those days if a policeman lost a prisoner he automatically lost his job. Everyone in the uniform in those times knew some unfortunate guy who had become a victim of this harsh reality. There were no excuses. If a prisoner was missing then the man who was responsible for the escort or the safe custody would soon be gone as well. The expression "down the road kicking frozen horse turds" reflected this reality.

A young constable was assigned to move a prisoner from the detachment lock-up at Meadow Lake to the prison at Prince Albert. The prisoner had been sentenced to ten days in custody for some minor offence. Meadow Lake Detachment where the sentence had been passed did not have long-term holding facilities so the prisoner escort was required. The prison at Prince Albert was and still is a federal penitentiary so the prisoner in this case would most likely have done his ten days in the police holding facilities there. Federal prisons were intended only for those who had been sentenced to two years or more.

The night before the escort was to be done there was a

# THE DIRTY THIRTIES ESCAPED PRISONER

farewell party for one of the policemen and the young constable attended and partied heartily. The man being transferred was a friend and had provided a lot of guidance to the young man who was on his first posting from the training facilities; he was going to miss this mentor.

Morning arrived and the young constable was somewhat the worse for wear. But he had known his assignment the day before and there was no begging off at this late hour. He gathered the required jail admission papers, placed his prisoner in the back of the police car and away they went. All went well until about the mid-point of the trip when some extreme intestinal discomfort demanded his urgent attention. He stopped the car by some scrub bush beside the road and was about to shackle the prisoner around a door post of the car when the prisoner convinced him that he too had to seek relief for a similar problem. The decision was made that they would both seek relief in the nearby bush. After all, the fellow was only going down for ten days, so surely he would not risk running from such a trivial matter. The policeman soon returned to the roadway and the car but the prisoner was nowhere to be seen. Panic reigned supreme. The realization that the prisoner was gone left no possibility that the young cop's pucker string could fail then.

After some vigorous searching and beating the nearby bush, the young policeman drove up and down the local roadways in the faint hope that he would spot his escapee, but to no avail. For the next while he circled the prairie blocks which were approximately one by two miles, clinging to the vague possibility that he may find the missing man. At the far end of one of these blocks he spotted a man just coming out of the bush alongside the road. At first he thought he was getting the big break he needed and that his prisoner was about to be captured again. No such luck! He did not recognize the man as he got closer but he decided to stop and ask if this fellow may have seen the escapee.

The man spoke only very limited English but it seemed that he had not seen anyone else that day. Further sign language and gestures were exchanged and the policeman learned that this fellow was hungry and without funds. The solution to both their problems came to the policeman immediately; he signed to the man that he would take him to a place where he could get three meals a day and could stay there for a little more than a week. The fellow was very appreciative; he became the stand-in for the missing prisoner and the young policeman kept his job. It seemed to be a win-win situation. The consequences, however, would have been much weightier if the facts had become known before the prisoner had "done his time."

According to the legend, the entire event unfolded as it had been planned in the brief moment of their chance encounter. From

## THE DIRTY THIRTIES ESCAPED PRISONER

many viewpoints it would have to be recalled as a "win – win" situation.

This tale adds a little more creditability to the old RCMP motto: *"The Mountie Always Gets His Man"* – or a reasonable facsimile thereof!

# Turkey
# Lessons

**A very valid question** in the policing world of today would be: *What would be the ideal background and upbringing for a prospective new member of the Royal Canadian Mounted Police, or for that matter any police establishment?* In my time I was of the firm opinion that a rural upbringing had many advantages over the urban one. Many lessons from my farm childhood served me well during my police career while dealing with people in the unimaginable variety of circumstances that police work presents. I, of course, being a prairie farm boy believed emphatically that the whole organization would crumble without the steady hands and valid input from those of us from that ideal rural background.

Many of us prairie farm boys who signed up in those times had some horse experience gained during our formative years of

# TURKEY LESSONS

farm work and our own recreation. This basic learning was of great benefit to us in the training stables and again when we began our actual work on the streets and roadways of our nation. Horses and people display a very surprising number of similarities but there are some traits in horses that do not show themselves so obviously in many human beings. The most outstanding of these is that horses will not knowingly plot or execute harm on one of their own or to a human being. The knowledge of how to react to the bluff and bluster of a horse was of great value to me in innumerable situations I encountered over the nearly twenty-eight years that I served with the Mounted Police. My horse experience had helped me to learn that under no circumstances should I allow myself to assume I could foresee or predict what a person might do during an encounter with me as a police officer.

I will now reveal a secret that I have carried with me for the many years of active service and nearly an equal time in my retirement. Though horses were important, the most valuable farm upbringing lessons that contributed to my successful police experiences came from a very surprising farm source – turkeys.

I was three years old when my father became the victim of a farming accident which left him a paraplegic for the rest of his life. This situation left my mother and my two older brothers – teenagers at that time – to take over and conduct a large mixed farming operation. I have no memory of the times when my father could walk but I do have many memories of the struggles our family went through to continue to make a living for all of us from our only material possession, the family farm.

My parents had always kept a small flock of turkeys. These mean and stupid creatures were tolerated because they provided a small source of cash when they were slaughtered and taken to market just before Christmas. The modest income enabled memorable Christmases with some little extras that would not

Being raised on a farm with working horses gave some of us a leg up during training in Ottawa. Note one horse (second from right) appears to be equipped with wide handlebars.

# TURKEY LESSONS

otherwise have been there. In the early times this required keeping about six turkey hens and a gobbler or "tom" so the hens could produce fertile eggs in the spring.

Turkeys were then and still are totally unpredictable and the breeding stock could very well be dangerous to small children like my sister and me. I clearly recall many times when the old tom would put the run on us, and the times when we were not quick enough and the "son-of-a bitch" would knock one of us down and proceed to peck and stomp us until our screams brought help from Mom or one of our big brothers. The danger to us "little ones" will have contributed to the decision to get rid of the breeding flock of turkeys and to replace them by buying day-old turkey poults from a commercial hatchery in the little town of Stony Plain. The task of bringing these stupid creatures to maturity was no easy undertaking but it did eliminate the mean-spirited breeding flock and the requirement to provide a warm place where that bunch could survive the prairie winters.

The day-old turkeys and chickens from the local hatchery were put in a small insulated farm building where a brooder stove provided the necessary warmth that would normally have been provided by the mother hen. These brooder stoves were a small cylindrical wood/coal burning unit fitted with a large inverted funnel-shaped hood that directed the heat toward the floor where the small birds were penned. The dry bedding required for the small birds made a very considerable fire hazard but thanks to some very careful supervision and operation by mother, we did not experience any fires. The new birds grew rapidly and in about six to eight weeks they would outgrow the need for the stove and the constant attention. This level of maturity in the new flocks soon allowed us to pen them in an outside area where they could learn to feed on grass and whole grain and they could perch overnight in the shelter of the many spruce trees that surrounded the farmyard.

Each young turkey represented a cash outlay and cash was a rare commodity; each one that met an untimely death was a blow to the operation. The turkeys taught us all to be constantly watchful and alert to dangers that only a turkey would find and take part in. On one occasion, Mother was preparing the brooder stove for the night. As she cleared the fire grate and shook a layer of glowing fire coals into the ash receptacle she removed the small iron door from the bottom/side of the stove and turned to reach the fire shovel to remove the hot ashes. Before she could turn back to the stove she smelled feathers burning and she found that one of her turkeys had run into the middle of this obvious glowing inferno and committed suicide. Another turkey lesson had been learned; any let down of your guard would be immediately taken advantage of.

After his accident and a period of healing, Dad's area of

# TURKEY LESSONS

the farm became the small patch of ground within the fence that surrounded the farm house and the garden area. On most warm summer days he struggled on his crutches around this one acre of ground while he tended to the garden and nurtured his honey bees and his orchard of crab apple trees. The turkeys were penned alongside the house-yard to keep them near enough to us to discourage coyotes and other predators yet far enough away to only expose us to some of the bad smells they generated.

On one of the warm and bright summer days, Dad was making his way along the fence near the turkey enclosure. His crab apple trees stood in a row along the fence and the trees had reached the point in their annual productive cycle where a natural thinning of the apple crop was happening. The ground was littered with small apples that had fallen during the "spring drop". As Dad moved along he collected these apples and tossed them through the wire fence where they were eagerly gobbled up by the turkeys. The turkeys obviously enjoyed these little treats and there was fierce competition among them for each tossed apple.

As the day wore on Dad moved along the row of crab apple trees and continued to toss the fallen apples to the eager turkeys. He moved slowly along until he reached one of his prized apple trees which produced apples at least twice the size of those from the other trees. One of the more aggressive and larger turkeys followed him very closely and continuously poked its head through

## WHEN GRAMPA WAS A MOUNTIE

the fence to get the jump on the others of the flock. When Dad reached the tree with the larger apples he wondered if the juvenile turkeys would be able to swallow this larger fruit. He selected one and presented it to the aggressive turkey with its head through the fence. The turkey immediately grabbed the apple and threw it to the back of its beak and tried to swallow it as he withdrew his head from the fence. Dad could see an immediate problem. There was a large bulge in the dumb critter's neck and the repeated swallowing attempts failed to move it. The eyes bulged and the colour drained from its head. In the next few moments the turkey sagged to the ground and it began to thrash around in a death struggle. Obviously it could not breathe with the apple in its neck. Dad could not get his crippled body over the fence to the bird, so all he could do was watch, all the while thinking he had killed the dumb fowl. He noticed the apple began to move as the death struggle continued and in a short time the apple slid into the crop at the base of the neck and the crisis was over. The colour began to return to the head and the stupid bird lay on the ground slowly blinking its eyes. In a few moments it was on its feet again and it immediately returned to the fence to again be the first to get the next apple.

Dad was always one to experiment; he was quite sure that particular turkey should have learned something from the near-death experience, but he had known these things for many years

## TURKEY LESSONS

and he had some genuine doubts. All things considered, the temptation to experiment was too much; he tossed it another apple. The turkey immediately grabbed it to prevent any other from getting it and then did an "encore performance" complete with the wing flapping and the loss of consciousness. The second experiment ended with the apple again moving into the crop and the bird eventually got to its feet to again stick its head through the fence.

Following that performance Dad crushed the remaining large apples between some boards and fed them apple sauce.

This was another "turkey lesson" – that stupidity knows no bounds! That farm boy knowledge served me well during my police career.

# Hope Beyond Hope

**There are many stories** about the adventures of RCMP members over the one hundred and forty years of history; each has significance to someone who was involved or was a near participant. Many of these adventures and experiences are being lost on a daily basis as the people who were involved go on to their final resting places. I have chosen a few of these incidents to write about in the hope that by doing so the heroics or just the day-to-day happenings will not be totally lost. This story is about an incident that happened during the evening of May 24, 1971. This tragedy nearly cost the life of a dedicated policeman. At the time of this happening, regimental number 21180 Constable Vernon Leslie "Vern" Mawhinney was stationed at Agassiz, BC where he worked as a highway patrol man.

Vern was born at Cut Knife, Saskatchewan on July 10, 1940. Primary school was completed there with several years

## HOPE BEYOND HOPE

of correspondence studies; correspondence was used because the rural schools in Saskatchewan in those times were staffed by teachers with minimal qualifications. Students attended the local schools but their studies were under the supervision of fully qualified teachers in the larger cities of the province; completed lessons were sent by mail and then graded and marked before being mailed back. When Vern was sixteen the family moved to Ontario where he attended high school and at the age of nineteen he joined the RCMP. After his training at Regina, Vern was transferred to Richmond, BC where he began his police career in earnest. During his early days at Richmond, Vern met a young lady and he and Magna soon realized that they were in love. They were married on September 8, 1962. They are the proud parents of Todd who was born in 1964 and Shannon who was born in 1967. During his time at Richmond; Vern found an interest in traffic law enforcement and he moved to the traffic section. He received training in patrol work with motorcycles and qualified for that duty along with other courses to do with this work.

The Mawhinney family had been transferred from Richmond to Hope several years before this happening. After their few years at Hope they were again transferred a short distance down the highway to Agassiz. In May of 1971, they were again in transfer mode and they had been working at painting and preparing their Agassiz home for sale before their next move to Golden,

## WHEN GRAMPA WAS A MOUNTIE

BC. A little side twist to this story was that my family and I were stationed at Golden at that time and we would have become workmates on completion of their pending move.

In that era, most of the BC highway system was tragically inadequate to cope with the rapidly ballooning population and traffic volume the province was experiencing. One of the most obvious bottlenecks in the whole province was at Hope where the Trans-Canada Highway intersected with BC Highway 3. Anyone who is sufficiently experienced with life in British Columbia (I mean you are old) will recall being in the Hope traffic jams or at least hearing the horror stories from friends who had been reluctant participants there. The weekend traffic volume at this junction was quite unbelievable; so much so that the motoring public made jokes about reaching a point in their travels where they were "beyond Hope". This quest to be "beyond Hope" applied to traffic in both directions, depending if you were on your way to the Interior at the start of a weekend or if you were trying to get home again to the Lower Mainland at the end of your weekend travels.

The RCMP detachment at Hope was responsible for trying to assist the motoring public with this huge lack of road facilities. The cops who got assigned to this duty were often subjected to a great variety of verbal abuse from frustrated motorists, some of whom seemed to actually believe that the police could have prevented part or all of the traffic congestion.

## HOPE BEYOND HOPE

One of the tools used to try to deal with this traffic mess was the police motorcycle. These machines were great for getting a policeman to the many secondary sites where the highway traffic prevented local traffic from crossing the highway or from getting into the line to wait their turn through the plugged intersections.

On the Monday afternoon of this happening, Vern had been asked to take the motorcycle from Agassiz detachment to Hope to assist with the routine traffic jam. Motorcycles have always been a cause for controversy in police circles; these machines have proven their worth in many instances but they have also been frequently involved in some very severe accidents. Over the years some RCMP detachment commanders have flatly refused to have a motorcycle unit in their jurisdiction, arguing that the potential for injuries and death outweighed the benefits of this equipment. The jury is still out on a final decision in this regard but motorcycles are still in use in many police organizations across North America.

The day of this incident was the end of a long weekend. The spring weather had been very nice and the motoring public had come out in record numbers. Vern had spent most of the afternoon trying to maintain some order in the heavy traffic near his home area and after dinner he arrived in Hope to assist there.

The best use of the available manpower was always a valid

concern so Vern was asked to assess the traffic volume waiting to get "beyond Hope". This information would assist with the decisions about manpower needs for the remainder of the day. He rode the motorcycle east along Highway 3 over a distance of more than eleven kilometres to where he had yet to find the end of the stalled line of traffic. During this ride he had issued traffic violations to several drivers who had amazingly tried to pass the unending line of other cars. He had warned several people of the danger of standing beside their cars because the much lighter Interior-bound traffic was still able to, and were, travelling at highway speeds.

Having learned the huge extent of the traffic volume, Vern turned back toward Hope. He rode near the centre line of the highway as he passed the long line of stopped cars. The emergency lights of the police motorcycle were displayed as he did this. As he neared the Hope area the traffic became more tangled by intersecting roadways and pedestrians and his speed had to be reduced. Having worked in Hope, he was quite familiar with the area but he had forgotten about an intersection where a roadway came up a steep hill from his right and onto the highway. A car and driver had been waiting to cross the highway from this steep roadway for some time. Finally a motorist in the stalled line of traffic had left a gap and the car moved forward to cross the highway.

Suddenly Vern was confronted by that car directly in his path, there was no time to react except to try turning to the left; in spite

# HOPE BEYOND HOPE

of this evasive action, he hit the car broadside. He and the motorcycle crashed and glanced off the car and into a rock-filled ditch beside the highway. Vern's first recollection of the incident is of him lying among the rocks near the motorcycle and the fact that he was partially sitting on the side of his long leather boot. He clearly remembers thinking that the position he was in was not possible. Extreme pain very quickly penetrated his shock and he knew that he was very badly injured.

The woman who was the driver of the car he had hit and a group of other people from the stalled traffic rushed to where he lay in the ditch. They all tried to assist but there was little or nothing that they could do. This happened long before the proliferation of cell phones so one of the people ran to a nearby motel and phoned for medical assistance and another police officer. A second policeman arrived quite quickly because he had been having his dinner at a nearby restaurant.

There was no local ambulance service in Hope at that time. Two of the four resident doctors were a husband and wife team who drove a full-size station wagon of their own. One of the other local doctors also drove a full-size station wagon; these doctor-owned vehicles were frequently pressed into ambulance duty and they undoubtedly had been responsible for the preservation of life for some of their patients. The doctors who drove and maintained these types of vehicles at Hope had learned how valuable these

## WHEN GRAMPA WAS A MOUNTIE

vehicles could be to their emergency patients and they made the vehicles available as an additional public service.

In a short time the husband of the doctor pair, Dr. Gerd Asche, arrived on the scene with his station wagon. The doctor gave Vern a shot of pain medication and then he began his preliminary assessment of the injuries. He quickly determined that Vern's right leg and foot were broken in five places; one above and three below the knee and a bone in his foot was also fractured. There was no time to lose; injuries of that extent will cause internal bleeding, severe shock and can very quickly lead to a death.

The doctor began the risky process of straightening Vern's body in preparation to get him onto a stretcher. The pain medication helped greatly but the process was excruciating and Vern wished he would pass out. With the help of bystanders, the doctor got him onto the folding stretcher and partly into the back of his station wagon for the short drive to the little hospital in Hope.

The wife of the doctor couple, Dr. Ursula Asche, met them at the hospital and they began the seemingly impossible task of stabilizing the shattered leg. A combination of splints and casts and traction were applied to hopefully get the broken bones into alignment and reduce the possibility of internal bleeding. A large and cumbersome hospital bed had to be used to aid with the traction and body support necessary for the stabilizing procedures.

# HOPE BEYOND HOPE

After several hours the doctors felt that the situation was stabilizing and there was some room for hope that Vern could survive his injuries. During all this Mag had been advised of the accident and that Vern was in the hospital at Hope. She arranged for a friend to look after their two small children and she drove there to be with him.

Early the next morning, during one of their many checks, one of the doctors became very concerned that Vern was showing signs of pneumonia. It seemed that he was progressing as well as could be expected but the doctor found some indications of breathing difficulties. The doctor made a note that special attention should be directed to his breathing. Early the following morning the doctors confirmed the presence of rapidly advancing pneumonia. The situation was discussed by the doctors and the local hospital administrator and they concluded that the only hope for survival was to move the patient to better equipped medical facilities at Shaughnessy Hospital in Vancouver.

The hospital administrator was a member of the RCMP Auxiliary group. He stepped in and requested assistance to evacuate Vern to Vancouver – a large twin rotor Search and Rescue helicopter was made available through "behind the scenes help" from the RCMP. The first contact with the crew of the helicopter brought the information that this large machine could not land anywhere near enough to the hospital to facilitate the direct

## WHEN GRAMPA WAS A MOUNTIE

transfer of the patient. A flatbed truck was volunteered from a local business operation, allowing the hospital bed to be loaded onto the truck and hauled to a nearby ball field where the helicopter was able to land. A railing had to be removed from near the doorway of the hospital so the bed could be gotten out and onto the truck. The huge bed was finally fitted into the helicopter and the doors were closed. Dr. Ursula Asche accompanied Vern on the helicopter ride to Vancouver.

On arrival at Shaughnessy Hospital they learned the bed would not fit into the elevator to take it to the intensive care unit on an upper floor. The lift was done in the freight elevator, after several attempts finally succeeded in fitting it all in.

Vern remained in the intensive care unit at Shaughnessy Hospital for sixteen days during which time the medical people applied a variety of drugs and lung drainage methods until the pneumonia subsided and he was moved to a regular ward. He had wondered why his visitors in the intensive care ward had never talked about his leg injuries. After he was back on the regular ward, his wife told him that the primary concern with everyone over the past two weeks had been his pneumonia.

Vern lay in full traction, flat on his back for two months until he was finally able to sit up and then to stand beside his bed. The long time without normal body movement had resulted in the formation of kidney stones which caused very severe pain, perhaps

# HOPE BEYOND HOPE

more severe than the original injuries in the crash. More medical intervention was finally able to clear this hurdle as well.

During the time in intensive care and specifically while the kidney stones were being treated, a blood clot developed in his uninjured leg but fortunately the doctors were able to dissolve it before it began to move about in his system.

After more than three months Vern was released from the hospital with a walking cast with steel pins through his ankle and just below his knee. A month later he returned to the hospital for a bone graft procedure as one of the breaks in his lower leg was not healing as it should.

It was just before the motorcycle crash that Mag and Vern had learned that their four-year-old daughter required urgent heart surgery to repair a defective valve. This additional matter was being attended to at the Vancouver General Hospital while Vern was back at Shaughnessy Hospital for the bone graft operation. This must have been wonderfully convenient for Mag as she could just scoot over the few blocks from the one hospital to the other to visit two of the most important people in her life. It seems that some of us are somehow blessed with better timing than others. Another positive happening during all this was the family move back to Richmond about the time Vern was released from the hospital for the first time. Mag's three months of long weekly drives from Agassiz with their children to visit Vern in the hospital were over.

One of the positive things from this whole adventure is that the little girl bounced back after the surgery and has enjoyed normal life ever since those trying times.

Another of the few bright spots in this complicated happening came when a group of the other RCMP members in the Agassiz area gathered together and finished the painting of the Mawhinney house.

Late in January the following year the casts were finally removed; Vern's leg had been saved but the injury has left him with severe walking difficulties to this day.

On March 3, 1972, Vern returned to light duties at Vancouver Town Station Detachment and he was back on regular duty by April 28, 1972. Eleven months had passed since the accident. The Mawhinney family was to have moved to Golden where Vern was to be promoted to corporal. This promotion was left on hold during his recovery; however, in Richmond he was able to return to full duty and he was promoted there about a year later than the original plan. He was again promoted at Richmond to the rank of sergeant in 1975. In 1986, they transferred to Victoria where Vern worked until he retired in 1993.

The RCMP can only be given a marginal grade for their help and support of one of their own at a critical time. The first correspondence that Vern can recall from the RCMP was a form letter which advised him that because he was not using his uniform

## HOPE BEYOND HOPE

while he was hospitalized he was no longer entitled to collect the money that was called "kit upkeep allowance", and therefore this eleven dollars would be removed from his monthly salary. Also his promotion to corporal was delayed by one year. There was some positive action in that his promotion to sergeant happened somewhat earlier than the average time for members in British Columbia during those times.

Throughout all the trials and tribulations these two have faced, Vern and Mag still look at the "good luck" and "good breaks" that have happened during their lives. They will point out that the crash was only about two blocks from the little hospital in Hope. The two doctors lived near the scene, they were both at home when it happened and these two were the Mawhinney family physicians. Mag had two sisters living in the Vancouver area at the time and they were a great help during the hospitalization and recuperation. These two provided child care, lodging, meals and moral support during a stressful time for Vern and Mag. Vern even sees his pneumonia as being responsible for his move to the larger and better equipped hospital in Vancouver where he had access to the best medical facilities in the province. My research into this happening has left me with the firm belief that the Mawhinney family is made up of some very strong and determined people. Canada or any nation on Earth would be greatly improved by the addition of more folks like these. Throughout

## WHEN GRAMPA WAS A MOUNTIE

their "life experiences", Mag has become an award-winning and very talented poet and songwriter; she writes about the "cowboy" and "homesteader" in our history and is quite well known among the many of us who cherish these memories.

# Lytton Weatherman Forecasts Extreme Heat

**Lytton was a very** small community but for reasons well beyond the knowledge of most of us, the Federal Government had established a weather reporting station there. The station was manned around the clock so there were four families living in the community to staff the facility. During holidays or if any of the full time staff were away; relief people were brought in for temporary duty from a variety of locations around the province. Lytton had achieved a bit of fame through the weather station in that the highest daytime temperature for all of Canada had been recorded there. The record temperature was 112 degrees F, and it had happened two days in a row on July 16 and 17, 1941.

The folks who worked at the weather station were a part of the community; most of them lived there with their families and took part in local events as we all did. One of the full-time weather staff members was a single man who took part in some community activities but to a lesser degree than his work mates. This fellow was often away to a variety of places during his days off, which was quite understandable in his bachelor circumstances. One of the married staff members had immediately joined the Lytton Volunteer Fire Brigade when he arrived there and was considered a good addition by the long-time volunteers. The people of the

Fire! Nature's fury, fanned by the canyon wind. Gusts would pick up flaming debris and fling it half a mile away to start another inferno in the tinder-dry forest.

## LYTTON WEATHERMAN
## FORECASTS EXTREME HEAT

little village were always looking for volunteers and the new man was made to feel welcome by the firefighters.

During our years in Lytton some strange and suspicious fires began to occur in the community. The high school which was located near the highway at the upper edge of the community was burned to the ground in a fire that broke out in the middle of the night. When the fire was first reported by a person passing by on the highway, the entire building was already involved.

The volunteer fire fighting service was called out by the wail of the siren on the firehouse. These dedicated men came quickly but when they arrived, the fire was beyond what the best equipped firefighters in the world could have put down. Their best efforts only managed to save the foundations.

The students suffered a loss that night along with the whole community. Almost every family had a member involved in some way as a student or with the operation and staffing of the school which was the largest facility in Lytton. The arsonist had truly struck at the heart of the community when he chose the high school.

It was fairly obvious to any observer that the fire had been intentionally started and at several locations within the structure. We had an arsonist on our hands, but who? And why would someone do such a thing? We at the police office were as baffled as anyone else in the community; we pondered the situation and our late night shift members were more vigilant.

## WHEN GRAMPA WAS A MOUNTIE

Hind-sight is always to the point and very accurate; the community was shocked when the arsonist was finally caught in the act after twenty-six suspicious fires over a two-year period. A historic home dating back to the very early days of Lytton was completely destroyed by one of these middle-of-the-night fires. Many fires took away older unoccupied homes and small outbuildings but each of them could have easily spread to occupied dwellings except for the efforts of the volunteer firemen. Two attempts were made on the community hall but for some strange reasons and some good luck the fires were reported in the very early stages and were put down before the building was lost.

Drawing on decades of experience, arson experts from the RCMP and the Provincial Fire Marshall's Office suggested that volunteer firemen should be carefully looked at as suspects. Once this process was underway the suspect almost jumped into our sights. There were many strong indications but nothing that was strong enough to bring him in for questioning so the decision was made to place him under surveillance. Additional manpower was brought in from other RCMP detachments and specialized units, and some assistance was made available through the office of the Fire Marshall. The process was extremely expensive but fortunately the man was soon caught in the act of starting another fire. He was observed placing and igniting a cardboard box filled with paper toweling. The paper in his "ignition box" was confirmed

## LYTTON WEATHERMAN
## FORECASTS EXTREME HEAT

to have come from the weather office where he worked. "The jig was up."

The volunteer firemen were more shocked than other citizens because they felt someone in their group should have become suspicious long before they did. Why did no one realize that the fires began with the arrival of their enthusiastic new volunteer who worked at the meteorological station? This man was most often the first to arrive in response to the siren and he would often have the equipment checked and the truck started before any others arrived. The fires had almost all started in the time between 2:00 and 3:00 a.m., and most happened while this man was on his all-night weatherman shift.

Our suspect "rode hard" on his right to remain silent but he pleaded guilty to the charges arising from the incident where he was caught in the act. In court, the crown prosecutor outlined the circumstances of all the other fires, much to the loud protests of the defence counsel who obviously felt that this man's rights were being ruthlessly trampled. The judge who heard the case seemed sufficiently convinced by all those circumstances and our man was sent up the "proverbial creek" for an extended period of time.

The suspicious fires stopped as abruptly as they had all started and the little community began to relax and enjoy its quiet existence once again, rain or shine.

# The Cost of Our Canadian Charter of Rights & Freedoms

**The sad news story** of the young man in the BC Lower Mainland who was shot and killed by the police in May 2013 raises some very valid questions. The police shooting happened within a few days of the lad killing two persons and then in another incident a day later he severely wounded a former landlord. The police came in contact with him after a citizen reported his whereabouts as a result of police requests for information. The young man jumped out of his van with a rifle in his hands knowing there were more than a dozen police officers surrounding him; this action was obviously a suicide however it seems he wanted to take more people with him. The police were forced to take a life; some of them will have to live with that fact.

About a year before this happening the young man had walked into a medical clinic in Victoria with the same rifle. The

## THE COST OF OUR
## CANADIAN CHARTER OF RIGHTS & FREEDOMS

police were called and were able to talk to him. Some excellent police work and some very good luck allowed the police to take possession of the firearm with no loss of life or injuries. However, the young man was not pleased he had lost his weapon and made this known. The police returned the weapon within about six weeks; apparently they felt no alternative based on their abundant experience in similar situations with a person's "charter rights". Later authorities from the office of the Chief Provincial Firearms Officer would dance a fine jig for the press and television people but none of them made any mention of the *Canadian Charter of Rights and Freedoms*. They did make the silly statement that they take their guidance from the police position on such happenings.

The firearm was returned because our modern society allows individuals to have extensive rights, without comparable levels of responsibility. The *Canadian Charter of Rights and Freedoms* grants many unquestionably valid rights but goes far beyond common sense. I am a believer in rights for individuals; however I was a police officer for decades and very often faced the awful results of someone taking full advantage of their Charter-enshrined rights. Rights are wonderful but they can come at a very high price to some of us: in this episode, three persons were dead and one more will never recover fully from his injuries, and police officers were forced to take a life while their lives were in danger.

The suggestion that we need more laws and regulation is not

the answer; the *Canadian Charter of Rights and Freedoms* and the modern application of its provisions is directly responsible for these tragedies. Our politicians and law makers should take a long and thorough look at this ugly fact even though such action will not generate votes.

A very telling aspect of this incident is the fact that not a single reporter from our abundance of press radio and television people felt any need to point to the *Charter of Rights and Freedoms* as being even vaguely responsible.

# Quesnel Wine Making, Featuring Mrs. Franco and Her *Grappa*

**This story begins in** the early summer of 1978 when we were transferred from Golden to Quesnel. We sold our lovely little home which was located on two town lots in a quiet corner of Golden and we were off to a new adventure in Quesnel. Real estate had begun the wild upward spiral which has been with us since those times with only a few minor slowdowns. We sold after having owned the home for five years to a son of the old couple we had bought the home from. We sold for $47,000 which was more than double the price we had paid.

Our third child and second son had arrived on the scene in the last weeks of our posting in Golden so he and his mother were very busy with the day-to-day requirements of a new born. With that situation in mind, I had driven to Quesnel alone to try to find a suitable home. I found almost nothing in the rental market but a good variety of nice homes for sale. I committed us to purchase one of these and we found it to be quite suitable during our four years there, in spite of the lack of spousal input.

During our years in Golden I had been introduced to the hobby of wine making. One of the many small shops in Golden was owned by a family who had contacts in the grape and wine businesses in the Okanagan Valley. Each fall this business owner arranged to bring a large truckload or more of grapes from the Okanagan and he would take orders from anyone in Golden who wanted to experiment with homemade wine. Any interested Golden residents would get in touch with this fellow and request their portion of the incoming grapes in the color and flavour mix of their preference. Deep discussions took place at his store about the weather in the Okanagan and the requirements for and the proper amount of irrigation to produce the best grapes. Many of us amateurs relished acting as "experts" in the production of grapes and wine during these conversations but the end result was always good wine at a reasonable price.

Patricia and I developed a taste for a half-and-half mix of dark red and white grapes. A very small cash outlay (though large in our budget) would give us enough grapes to produce about five gallons of excellent wine.

## QUESNEL WINE MAKING, FEATURING
## MRS. FRANCO AND HER *GRAPPA*

During our first weeks in Quesnel I asked around the police office if there was a similar business operation there and I was directed to Franco's Delicatessen on Front Street. On my next day off I went to Franco's and was greeted by a very pleasant lady who was, by her accent, obviously of Italian origin. We had a nice visit and I learned that she and her husband owned and operated the little business and that Franco also worked full-time at a local mill. His days off from his mill job became ten- to twelve-hour shifts in the store business where he looked after stock ordering, record keeping and some heavy lifting as they rearranged their inventory to keep a fresh appearance in their shop. Neither of these two had a lazy bone in their bodies.

During this first visit, Mrs. Franco and I discussed the art of wine making and she suggested a few tricks her ancestors had learned for me to apply to my next batch. The grape order book was brought out and an entry was made to ensure that I would receive my order of quality grapes from the first available Okanagan shipment.

During our visit, Mrs. Franco poured us two small stem glasses of beautiful red wine and then brought out a chunk of hard cheese from one of the store coolers. The combination of the wine and cheese presented a taste experience that I was totally unprepared for. The wine was from their production, very rich red and very dry. The cheese was Parmigiano-Reggiano – very hard and crumbly. Please consider this as a warning that should you chose to try this combination, you may find that you lack of the necessary will-power to stop.

As our first summer in Quesnel passed I was in the Franco Store on several occasions when I purchased small grocery items and visited again with the couple. Without any deliberate plan in mind, I had been in civilian dress on every occasion that I went to their store. About six weeks after our first meeting I happened into the store on a day when Franco was at work. I was again not in uniform. Mrs. Franco and I talked about wine making and the current weather conditions in the Okanagan area and how the weather has a large influence on the quality of grapes all over the globe.

During this visit I opened the topic of *"grappa"*. Grappa is an Italian word for the product that is produced by the distillation of second run wine. The private distillation of any alcohol product is very much against the law in Canada but obviously our frequent meetings had wrongly convinced Mrs. Franco that I could not possibly be "one of those." She asked if I would like a sip of grappa and poured a very small quantity into two tiny glasses and we toasted our good health. Unlike the Franco wine and cheese combination, this taste experience was purely medicinal. I still believe that there were small blue flames around my nose and mouth but I tried to be "manly" and I indicated that it was good even though my knees were a bit wobbly. The tiny

## QUESNEL WINE MAKING, FEATURING
## MRS. FRANCO AND HER *GRAPPA*

grappa container was again stored carefully away in its secret location.

The enforcement of the law in regard to distillation is one of the many facets of law that are not vigorously pursued by most Canadian police agencies. It is fairly common knowledge that many ethnic groups do this on a very limited basis and the product is used only for private enjoyment. In any situations where there is some indication that the distilled products are being marketed or distributed, the law will be applied to the full extent of police resources.

After leaving the store I thought about what had happened and I formulated an evil plot. I had not realized until that moment that I had not been in the store in uniform and my work had never become a topic of our conversations. This combination of circumstances left a situation which I could not let pass.

The next day I was back at work and telling one of my constables about the grappa experience and about my evil plot. He insisted on being in on it so the two of us barged into the Franco shop in uniform. As the little bell clattered above the entrance door Mrs. Franco looked up from whatever she was doing at the moment. She looked at me for only the brief moment that I was able to keep a straight face and she immediately went into shock. Her eyes opened to beyond what could be described as wide. She made odd jerky movements with her arms and hands as she walked in a tight ever-shrinking circle. In what was fortunately a very brief time she became aware that we were both laughing and she began to calm down.

As soon as she had regained most of her composure we carried on with a short visit. I felt I had to deliver a bit of a warning about the grappa incident and she immediately promised that it would be removed from the store and never again offered to strangers. She brought out a bit of Parmigiano-Reggiano but no wine. The cheese with no wine left me to regret what I had just done.

# The Fred Quilt Frame-up: two constables ensnared in a tangle of pent-up resentment and orchestrated lies

**Alexis Creek in 1971** was a small settlement in the middle of the vast Chilcotin region of central British Columbia. The village consisted of the Hitching Post hotel/motel, two typical small town grocery stores, the post office, a community hall and a two-room school house, surrounded by a loose assortment of homes. Access to those homes was by gravel-surfaced short streets branching off the main drag which was Highway 20.

The Chilcotin region was named for the Chilcotin First Nation that has existed in this area since well before recorded history began. The Anaham Indian Reserve (the legal name is Anahim's Flat Indian Reserve #1) was eight kilometres to the east of Alexis Creek.

## WHEN GRAMPA WAS A MOUNTIE

During the early seventies only the most determined travelers would attempt the drive across the Chilcotin Plateau on Highway 20, 470 kilometres of rough and tough, winding dirt and gravel road between Williams Lake on the east and Bella Coola to the west. (It has since been greatly improved and black-topped.) Anyone doing so in a conventional road vehicle was well advised to have spare wheels, tires, tools and extra parts plus some basic mechanical understanding and expertise to allow for minor repairs and maintenance along the way.

Alexis Creek at that time had a population of about 250 people (mostly whites) and it was the largest settlement on the entire route, serving as a trading hub for the Chilcotin region. Williams Lake, more than two hours drive to the east, was and still is the trading centre of the entire Cariboo region. Bella Coola is on Pacific tide water at the head of a long inlet.

The Alexis Creek RCMP detachment was a three-man operation with a corporal in charge. The detachment building stood at the edge of the little community. One side of the wood frame structure was the typical office facilities while the other side served as living quarters for the man in charge and his family. Directly behind the police building stood a double-wide house trailer, with another, single-width trailer nearby. The double-wide was provided by the RCMP as rental accommodation for the

## THE FRED QUILT FRAME-UP

second policeman and his family; the smaller trailer was rented to an unmarried police officer.

Alexis Creek and Williams Lake were separated by 120 kilometres of road that was rough going in the best weather and near impassible in bad. This geographical fact left the RCMP at Alexis Creek with an additional problem not entirely unique in the overall policing of the British Columbia interior region. They had some limited lock-up facilities but the finding of guards and matrons nearby was almost impossible as most responsible citizens had full time work. The long haul to Williams Lake was sometimes forced upon the officers when the custody of some person became unavoidable.

Corporal J.J. "Jack" Hest was in charge of Alexis Creek Detachment at the time of this story. Jack was an experienced police officer, having served in a variety of locations around the province. He was a man who enjoyed the isolated location, with the additional responsibilities and the challenges that accompanied it.

Jack couldn't have foreseen the tragic events to come, nor the devastation about to happen to two members of the RCMP and their families, and the unfair tarnishing of the Force's reputation. Two policemen would be falsely accused of a brutal crime. Neither of these two policemen did anything wrong in this situation; they had simply answered the call of duty as they had been doing since taking the oath upon joining the Force. They both paid a terrible price. These two men had absolutely nothing to do with the historical or current situations faced by the Native Indians of this region; however they became entangled in a morass of pent-up ill-will, revenge, political correctness and shame that delayed and thwarted justice.

This story is one that has needed telling for many years. It may seem 'politically incorrect' to some. Yet it cannot be told without being critical of some Native individuals; the facts of this event can lead only to the conclusion that the people who took part were not only wrong in their conduct and deportment, they also committed a variety of criminal offences which had devastating effects on two innocent victims. The Canadian justice system in its need to be perceived as 'politically correct' allowed two constables to be judged guilty by Native Rights activists and the international media.

During my decades of police service I came to know many Native people, and I am quite sure that the majority of them would not have taken part in the main happening of this story. Native pride and their genuine sense of decency would not allow most of them to be involved in such an injustice.

Many conversations with my workmates over the last half of my service focused on the horrors of this event and the damage it caused to the two policemen and their families. The allegations

# THE FRED QUILT FRAME-UP

were amplified to the print and broadcast media by an impromptu committee of Natives who came together for the specific purpose of doing as much damage to these men and to the RCMP as they could possibly accomplish. The Native accusers took full advantage of the weakness displayed by the senior management of the RCMP, the Canadian Court system and the misinformed Canadian population in general. Both constables were "born and raised Canadians" from several generations of Canadian ancestors. Fate alone put these two unfortunate men into the path of this conspiracy – it could very easily have been me or any other policeman serving in the Force during that era.

Perhaps the telling of the details of this incident will bring some small measure of comfort to the surviving family and friends of Constables Peter Eakins and Daryl Bakewell. The facts have been far too long in getting out. The ancient Chinese religion of TAO contained a great variety of thoughts and practices with deep meaning for all of mankind. One of their cornerstones was the belief that every event or happening among humanity would be a multi-faceted event and that any subsequent thought or consideration would require a thorough search and examination of every possibility that may or did effect the specific situation. We should look at both sides of every event or in many situations look at many facets or possibilities before we form a solid opinion.

It was late Sunday afternoon, November 28, 1971, when the

public health nurse from Alexis Creek phoned the RCMP member on duty, Constable Peter Eakins. She reported there was an old pick-up truck sitting in the middle of the road without its lights on near the Anaham Indian reserve. The vehicle was just over the crest of a hill on a curve, and there were four people in it who were all quite obviously intoxicated, according to the nurse. Peter took the report while having a meal with his wife and young family at his home. Constable Daryl Bakewell was a dinner guest and offered to attend the call with Peter. The two young constables left the village for the short drive to where the people and vehicle had been reported. Neither man had any thoughts that this routine call would lead them into a vicious conspiracy that would haunt them for the rest of their lives.

Back in the late 18th century, fur trader Alexander Mackenzie, while on an exploratory trip down the Fraser River, branched away from the Fraser and crossed the Chilcotin Plateau from a point near the confluence of the Fraser and Blackwater rivers. Mackenzie reached Pacific tidal water at Bella Coola on July 20, 1793; he then returned to the Fraser River by the same route. Mackenzie's party followed the traditional Native trading route known as the *grease trail*. The interior Natives made their way annually to the Bella Coola area to trade for fish oil with the coastal Indians. This fish oil was a dietary supplement vital to the survival of the Chilcotin,

# THE FRED QUILT FRAME-UP

Carrier and Shuswap Indians in the harsh winter conditions of their inland territories.

Mackenzie's diaries mentioned aggressive Natives he encountered near Bella Coola but it would seem he did not have any noteworthy encounters with the Natives of the Chilcotin area even though he passed through the middle of their territory in both directions. His peaceful passage is somewhat of a mystery as nearly all other early accounts of the region describe the "aggressive nature" of the Chilcotin Indians. In contrast, the Shuswap First Nation that was centred in the area to the south and east of the Chilcotin, and the Carrier First Nation that existed mainly to the north, were much more accommodating to the white explorers and traders as they began to appear in their territories, more inclined to welcome the invaders with their trade goods. My own theory about the mystery of Mackenzie's peaceful hike across the plateau is that his mid-summer trip must have coincided with the annual run of Pacific Sockeye salmon into the Fraser and Chilcotin Rivers, terminating in Chilko Lake. During this annual happening, all the able-bodied Chilcotin Natives would have been fishing in the Farwell Canyon well to the south east of Mackenzie's route. Only the very old, very young, and infirm tribe members would have remained in their traditional areas to observe the passage of the white strangers and to tell the story to the others on their return. If my theory is correct, Mackenzie may well have been the benefactor of some very lucky but accidental timing.

The greasy fish oil referred to in the name *grease trail* was produced by the Bella Coola Indians from a small ocean fish known as the eulachon or candle fish. The term *candle fish* comes from the fact that these little fish are so oily that the dried carcass of one can be stuck in the sand and lighted with a match whereupon it will slowly burn away. The eulachon came into the coastal estuaries to spawn in such great numbers that the Natives were able to scoop them out of the river in millions with the use of dip nets with netting crafted from braided roots and cedar bark fibre. The fish were dumped into large containers formed of animals hides or tightly-woven cedar fibre. The catch was then basically left to rot in these containers. During the rotting process the abundant oil floated to the surface and was scooped off and stored in leather bags or in the visceral organs of animals the Natives had hunted for food. The grease trail was no doubt in existence for hundreds and perhaps thousands of years before Mackenzie's time. There were, of course, no written records of the trade among the Natives along the grease trail but it is believed that the interior Natives took dried meat and animal hides to trade for the oil so vital to their survival.

The Chilcotin was in 1971, and still is, a land of ranchers, loggers, Natives, cowboys, legends and legendary people. Many

# THE FRED QUILT FRAME-UP

have heard of the Gang Ranch (with over a million acres, once the largest spread in North America) and stories from the Hanceville, Farwell, and Big Creek areas.

One of the most famous stories is about the "Chilcotin War" which took place in the spring and summer of 1864. Gold was discovered in the central Cariboo in late 1860. In 1862, construction crews began working from Bute Inlet on the Pacific Coast up the Homathco River Valley on what was intended to be a better access route to the gold fields via an overland route northeast across the Chilcotin plateau. Smallpox reached the Chilcotin at about the same time and the disease was devastating to the Natives, who had no prior exposure to this or similar germs and therefore no acquired immunity. Entire communities were wiped out. In response to threats of further spread of smallpox and other alleged wrongs by the whites, in 1864 a group of Chilcotin Natives banded together in a "war party" and began a systematic expulsion and, in some cases, slaughter of non-Native men in the western portion of the region. This action resulted in about twenty deaths of settlers and workmen. The following year the Native warriors were tricked into attending a faked negotiation meeting with the colonial governor, then promptly arrested. Five of their number were tried and then hanged.

Bitterness and resentment about their war, the horrific smallpox devastation, residential school abuse, banning of their religion and traditions, and other perceived injustices were certainly and understandably present among these people in the early 1970s. This mind-set will no doubt have contributed to some of the actions by the Quilt group in this story; however, another aspect of the actions of Christine Quilt had no background or bearing whatever in the invasion of her homeland.

A deep disdain for the "whiteman's authority" was present across the region, and was evident in acts of vandalism and discontent. For example, there were reports to the police of cattle having been shot and left to rot on the non-Native Chilcotin range lands; sometimes a portion of the shot animals had been cut away. The police at Alexis Creek detachment found no evidence pointing to a suspect or suspects in these cattle killings; the lack of co-operation from the Natives made investigations very difficult and mostly non-productive.

I served at the Williams Lake detachment from 1967 to 1969 and can remember we were experiencing a plague of stolen vehicle reports. However, unlike most police jurisdictions in Canada, almost none of the missing vehicles were being recovered. One day, a helicopter pilot happened to notice a cluster of burned out vehicles in a ravine just off the edge of the Anaham Reserve community. He reported this sighting to the RCMP. Investigators discovered the charred remains of most of the approximately one hundred vehicles that had gone missing from Williams Lake

## THE FRED QUILT FRAME-UP

during the preceding few years. The heap of destroyed vehicles had accumulated over several years and was so near the homes of the reserve that nearly all, if not all, of the residents had to be aware of it. Police investigations attempting to identify the persons responsible for the theft and burning of the vehicles met no success. None of the reserve residents would answer our questions about the destruction of the vehicles, let alone name or implicate any possible suspects. The files were eventually closed without conclusion.

The Anaham Reserve, sadly like many other Native settlements, at times descended into being a morass of alcohol abuse and despair, a living hell for everyone living there. Addicts drank whatever liquor they could obtain as fast as they could pour it into their bodies: they also consumed rubbing alcohol, shaving lotion, vanilla extract, melted shoe polish, Lysol spray, Sudden Beauty Hair Spray, and many commonly available household cleaning agents.

*(Since first contact with Europeans, the North American Natives have been known to have an inability to deal with the power of alcohol and this major problem led to the rise of the whiskey trading business on the Prairies soon after the first explorers and traders arrived there. The magnitude of and the need to control this problem became obvious to the Canadian government after the massacre of Indians by American whiskey traders*

## WHEN GRAMPA WAS A MOUNTIE

*at Cypress Hills, and was largely responsible for the formation of the Royal Canadian Mounted Police in 1873.)*

The police investigation of almost any matter arising on such reserves was an almost impossible task. The effects of generations of ill-will and mistrust could not be swept aside no matter how diplomatic a policeman might be. Nonetheless, we policemen had a sworn duty to defend the law, without fear, favour or affection, wherever we were required to attend.

Such was the situation facing the two constables who answered that call on November 28, 1971. Peter Eakins and Daryl Bakewell found the people and the vehicle as had been reported. There were no lights working on the old truck and it was just over the crest of a hill on a curve. Traffic at that location and at that time of night was almost non-existent but there was an obvious need to remove these people from this dangerous situation and to clear the roadway. It appeared some mechanical failure had stopped the old truck, after which the occupants, in their advanced state of intoxication, had tried to restart it until the battery was completely dead.

There were four Native persons in the truck. Three of the four later argued, while under oath, that there had been five of them in the truck and they described a variety of seating arrangements and named a young man who accounted for the fifth person. In spite of this glaring demonstration of their inebriated condition, each

## THE FRED QUILT FRAME-UP

of them later insisted while under oath at two coroner's inquests, that they had had very little or nothing to drink.

The smell of the people in the old truck told the constables that the major portion or all of what they had been drinking was vanilla extract. There were five 16-ounce vanilla extract bottles in the cab of the truck. One was empty, one partly empty, and three full and capped. Daryl gathered the bottles and smashed them on rocks at the side of the road. Such a course of action was certainly not in keeping with the policies and instructions of the RCMP; but this was the Chilcotin; time and manpower did not always allow for the detailed handling of every administrative aspect of policing. The vanilla should have been seized and carried back to the police office where multiple copies of exhibit reports would have to be completed and labels applied to each article before they were stored in the secure exhibit locker. If either Peter or Daryl had been able to foresee the convoluted aftermath of this seemingly routine incident they would no doubt have paid much more attention to such details.

The vehicle was owned by a well-known couple from the isolated Stone Reserve, Fred and Christine Quilt, and they were both present in the disabled truck. The Stone Reserve lies about 30 kilometres south of the Anaham Reserve and on the opposite side of the Chilcotin River. The other two people in the disabled truck were Agnes Quilt, a sister-in-law of Christine, and Robin Quilt,

# WHEN GRAMPA WAS A MOUNTIE

a 19-year-old son of Christine whom Fred had adopted. The fifth person who was there only in their alcohol-clouded imaginations was another young Native man from the Stone Reserve. This person was interviewed later and he stated that he had been with the Quilt group on the drive from the Stone Reserve to Anaham Reserve but he had left their company to visit with others at the reserve shortly after they all arrived.

The Stone Reserve was much more isolated than Anaham and the Native lifestyle there was subjected to far less interference from the dominant white society, their police and laws. The Fred Quilt family apparently preferred this more open, do as you wish, lifestyle and they frequently came into conflict with the law when they ventured away from their more tolerant home area. Conflict was almost a certainty when they ventured into Alexis Creek or Williams Lake. At the Anaham Reserve, there were resident employees of the Indian Affairs Department and staff from the Roman Catholic Church who would call the Alexis Creek RCMP with complaints over behaviour by the Quilts that might have been looked on at the Stone Reserve as routine conduct. This reporting to the police was apparently considered by the Quilts as another unjustified and unwelcome interference by the dominant white society.

Fred Quilt had been involved as a student in the government-funded and church-operated residential school system, but his

## THE FRED QUILT FRAME-UP

wife Christine had somehow evaded it. Fred was able to read and write and he spoke English quite well. Christine was illiterate and had limited speaking ability and understanding of English. She definitely preferred to speak her Native language. Christine had given evidence in British Columbia courts as a witness but this was always done through an interpreter. Christine's experience and understanding of the legal system would soon be put to use in a devious and vicious attack against two innocent victims.

Fred Quilt was well known among the police of the Chilcotin and Cariboo regions as a quite overweight man who frequented any and all sources of liquor, or alcohol in any form. He traveled the roads of the entire area much more than most of his peers. He was most often in possession of a vehicle of some type and his vehicles were always a marvel of neglect and disrepair. Although he listed his profession on government documents as *ranch hand*, Fred had no permanent employment and relied largely on whatever funds were available through his band.

*The Forestry Act* of British Columbia allowed for conscripting any able-bodied person to fight forest fires whenever the need arose. Fred would occasionally be conscripted by the provincial forest service under this legislation. I recall conversations with men from the Cariboo district of the British Columbia Forest Service about their fire experiences and the name Fred Quilt often came up in these discussions. It seemed that Fred was a very beneficial member on the fire lines; he worked hard, was alert and could often anticipate the best way to quell a fire. Apparently he thoroughly enjoyed the challenge of a fire and the camaraderie of the fire lines. Yet when Fred was relieved or finished his duty on the fire fighting lines and received his wages, he always came into a clash with the law as he set about spending his new-found wealth on a no-holds-barred drinking binge.

During this 1960s–1970s era, we policemen observed that Native people generally drank beer in the less trendy beer parlors of the interior British Columbia towns. If they purchased liquor for consumption at home or on the street, their choice was almost exclusively cheap wine. This selection was apparently made because experience had taught them that this product was compatible with all-out binge drinking. Beer was low in alcohol content and required relatively large volumes to produce the desired intoxication. Distilled liquor is dangerous in that it can be lethal by alcohol overdose in a frenzied drinking situation. Cheap wine was ideal because one received the maximum effect for each dollar yet the alcohol content was low enough to very seldom result in death by alcohol poisoning.

Fred Quilt had developed an amazing, near legendary, tolerance for alcohol. His larger than average body bulk no doubt contributed greatly to his ability to remain upright in spite of an overload of alcohol. Police noted that whenever Fred had sufficient

## THE FRED QUILT FRAME-UP

funds he would buy one or several small bottles of whiskey along with his wine. He poured the wine into himself with wild abandon but he would sip carefully from the whiskey at the same time. Decades of experience and practice had taught him to manage this successfully. Fred was also known among his peers for frequently bringing a small concealed bottle of whisky into the beer parlors. He would spike his beer from his secreted stash and would become intoxicated in a much shorter time than his companions.

On one of Fred Quilt's occasional visits to Williams Lake, the police had encountered him driving his vehicle erratically. He was arrested and a demand for a breath sample was made as a matter of routine. I administered the breath test that indicated a blood alcohol content [BAC] level of 400 milligrams of alcohol in 100 millilitres of blood, a remarkable .40 percent BAC. A reading of .08 percent blood alcohol is considered by law to prove legal impairment of a person's ability to drive a vehicle. At .30 percent, death is possible. A blood alcohol level in the .40 percent range or even considerably lower was typically found only in a corpse yet Fred Quilt was still able to walk and talk and function to some extent. For this man to be conscious and somewhat functional with such an alcohol level, he had to be among the most conditioned and practiced of alcohol abusers.

Later investigation into the source of the vanilla extract the Quilts had been drinking on that November 1971 evening led to a

# WHEN GRAMPA WAS A MOUNTIE

country store at Hanceville on the road between the Anaham and Stone reserves. The records kept by the storekeeper showed that the Quilt family group had purchased more than ten bottles of this product in the few days prior to this encounter. The sale or supplying of such products to Natives was under some vague legal control method at that time and the storekeeper was questioned under that legislation. The response to the policeman was very straightforward and to the point: "I can sell it to them or I can get my store burned out!" No enforcement action was brought against the storekeeper.

To tell the full story, there is another character to be introduced, someone involved in a related frame-up, but living "as a guest of the Queen" in prison in November of 1971. Stephen Hink was a member of the Stone Reserve community and neighbour of the Quilt family. He and his kin and friends lived from day to day around the reserve; their most notable contribution to the community was to go on an occasional hunt for deer or moose. Traditionally, success on a hunt would have resulted in a celebration, bringing the community together for a "potlatch". Such events had been frequent occurrences over the thousands of years the Chilcotins had lived in that part of the world. Unfortunately, since the arrival of the white settlers, alcohol has become the bane to these gatherings. A successful hunt would inevitably turn into a violent group alcohol binge where one or more of the celebrants

# THE FRED QUILT FRAME-UP

might die in some senseless alcohol-induced misadventure. After one such celebration in December of 1968, Stephen Hink awoke to find himself in police custody accused of having shot and killed a woman who had been one of his reserve neighbours, Rose Setah. Hink was so drunk at the time of the killing that he had no memory of the event whatever. He couldn't deny what others accused him of, since he couldn't remember a thing. On the basis of a witness's testimony, Hink was arrested and charged with murder; he was tried and convicted of manslaughter in the BC Supreme Court at Williams Lake and sentenced to life in prison. The majority of the evidence against Hink was provided by witness Christine Quilt through an interpreter. Christine gave sworn testimony that she had seen Stephen Hink deliberately fire the fatal shots with a .22 calibre rifle. Hink would serve three years in the Canadian penitentiary system before he was granted parole. The strict conditions of his parole required that he was to live on the Stone Reserve, abstain from alcohol consumption and be of good behaviour. He was not to leave his home area without the permission of his parole officer and these conditions were to remain with him for the rest of his life.

On November 28, 1971, when the two constables from the Alexis Creek detachment found the vehicle and people as had been reported to them, Constable Peter Eakins opened the driver's door of the old pick-up. He found Fred Quilt slumped behind the

183

WHEN GRAMPA WAS A MOUNTIE

steering wheel. Peter tried to awaken Fred and get him out of the vehicle but there was no response. He grasped Fred by the shoulders and started to move him toward the open door which resulted in Fred partially dropping to the ground beside the truck. The legs of the obese man remained in the cab until his buttocks were on the ground. Peter testified at the two inquests that he had held Fred's head and shoulders as best he could until the entire body was in a prone position on the ground beside the truck. Fred had vomited in the truck at some time before the police arrived. There was vomited matter on the front of his clothing and on the seat and steering wheel. This fact was not made an issue at the subsequent inquests although it should have been; Fred Quilt was a very conditioned alcohol abuser and most certainly not prone to stomach upset from the consumption of vanilla extract or any other source of ethyl alcohol. There should have been consider-able suspicion about the cause of his upset stomach. As the story unfolded some years later, the real cause became quite clear.

After removing Fred Quilt from the driver's position, Peter went to the passenger side of the truck and began removing the other three intoxicated people from the cab. Constable Daryl Bakewell stepped in to try to move Fred into the police vehicle, which was parked close behind the Quilt truck. Fred was not very responsive and Daryl swore at Fred as he tried to assist him to his feet to move the few yards. After Daryl managed to assist him to

## THE FRED QUILT FRAME-UP

a standing position beside his truck, Fred held onto the side of the truck box and resisted being moved. Daryl pulled to break Quilt's hold, an action which resulted in them both falling to the ground when Quilt's hold on the truck box was suddenly released. Daryl tried again to get Fred to his feet but finally had to drag the fat fellow to the police vehicle. As they reached the police vehicle Fred seemed to awaken somewhat and cooperated with being put into the back seat of the four-door pick-up truck that was the Alexis Creek patrol vehicle.

When Peter Eakins reached the police vehicle with the other three persons he found Fred Quilt was already in the truck. Immediately after assisting the remaining three into the back of the police truck, the two constables attempted to push the disabled Quilt truck to the edge of the road but they were unable to move it by hand. They then realized the tow cable normally carried in their vehicle was missing and they recalled that it had been left at their office in Alexis Creek. The police truck was equipped with a cable winch on the front bumper but this piece of equipment was broken and the necessary parts were on order through the dealer in Williams Lake.

Because the Quilt group lived on the Stone Reserve about 30 kilometres away from the location of their arrest, the two constables decided they would seek some alternative to driving them to their home. Earlier that same day during one of his patrols,

WHEN GRAMPA WAS A MOUNTIE

Peter had seen the Quilt vehicle near a residence on the nearby Anaham Reserve and had assumed there was a family or friendship connection with the occupants of that home. The decision was made to release the prisoners there, assuming that they would find shelter with friends or relatives. The police cells at Alexis Creek were capable of holding this group but it was a Sunday evening and finding a citizen who would guard the cells for the night would be very difficult if not impossible. The fact that there were women among the prisoners would require the hiring of a matron in addition to the guard, increasing the challenges of finding available and suitable people. Most of the responsible citizens of the area had full time work or child-minding obligations, and therefore would not come in on short notice and stay awake all night for the minimal pay that was available as a cell guard. These circumstances contributed to the decision to take the drunks to the nearby reserve home and release them there.

Harry Rankin, a well-known Vancouver lawyer, made a great issue of the release of the Quilts at the Anaham Reserve during the second inquest held at Kamloops. Rankin was extremely critical of the two officers for releasing these people in their drunken condition. He alternated between suggesting that they were not really drunk or that they should definitely not have been released in the condition the constables described.

In the times before the European invasion of the native lands

## THE FRED QUILT FRAME-UP

the word *potlatch* referred to a ceremonial event where a tribe gathered to mark an event by the giving of gifts and feasting. Unfortunately, since contact with whites and their alcohol, community gatherings became all-out drinking binges. There was a funeral potlatch underway at the Anaham Reserve that night and as in every such event there was a huge drinking binge.

If this happening was anything like the many such events that I witnessed over my years in policing then I suspect there may have been only a handful of persons in the entire reserve population who, under ideal circumstances, should not have been placed in protective custody because of their extreme drunken condition.

The short drive from the stalled truck to the reserve was uneventful except for the four drunks complaining they felt they were being picked on. They were all verbally abusive to the constables. Both policemen had been stationed in Alexis Creek for some time and they were quite familiar with the layout of the Anaham Reserve. They drove quickly over the short distance onto the reserve to get rid of their abusive and foul-smelling passengers. They pulled up near the home where Peter had seen the Quilt vehicle earlier that same day, and the four passengers were assisted out of the police vehicle. As the group walked away from the police vehicle, Christine Quilt said, "Thanks for the ride."

The constables watched the four stagger off toward the nearby house until they were quite satisfied that these people were about

WHEN GRAMPA WAS A MOUNTIE

to enter the house. During the short ride to the reserve, Fred Quilt made no reference or complaint about the way he had been dealt with by the two constables and Christine and the others made no mention of the extreme violence they would testify about at the subsequent inquests.

The constables drove back to the disabled truck and placed an incendiary flare on the roadway on each side of it. They then drove back to Alexis Creek to get the tow cable from their office. They expected the 20-minute burn time of the flares would give them time to get the cable and return so they could drag the vehicle to a safer location. There were no commercial tow trucks available in the Alexis Creek area at that time. Any tow vehicle would have to come from Williams Lake. Had this been requested, the disabled vehicle would have been hauled back to Williams Lake resulting in serious inconvenience and considerable cost to the vehicle owner.

The policemen were delayed by other matters in Alexis Creek. It was nearly an hour later when they again approached the location of the stalled truck. As they approached the area they were able to see from more than a kilometre away the glow in the sky of a large fire. On arrival they discovered the truck was over the edge of the roadway and burning vigorously. Christine Quilt and two young men were standing on the road near the burning

## THE FRED QUILT FRAME-UP

truck. As the constables reached the scene, Christine Quilt immediately accused them of setting fire to the truck.

The two constables had been unable to move the truck to a safer location because that action required pushing the vehicle up a slight incline to a place where the narrow shoulder would partially accommodate it. To get the vehicle downhill over the edge of the road to where it was burning required very little effort; it may have rolled there by its own weight after simply releasing the emergency brake and taking it out of gear.

Later the same evening a phone call was received by Corporal Jack Hest at the Alexis Creek detachment. The call was from a nursing sister at the Catholic Mission on the Anaham Reserve. The sister had been summoned to the home where Fred Quilt was and she had found him to be in severe pain. He complained of pain in his chest and she thought he may have broken or cracked ribs. She had given him some medication for the pain but she felt he was in need of medical attention. Jack knew an ambulance was coming out from Williams Lake the next morning and he arranged to contact the ambulance crew and have them attend and assess Quilt's condition and take whatever action they deemed necessary. The nursing sister was called as a witness at both subsequent inquests; she gave evidence of her being called to the home where she talked with and examined Fred Quilt. It is of interest that Fred made no mention to this woman about the extreme violence he would later

# WHEN GRAMPA WAS A MOUNTIE

claim to have suffered at the hands of these two policemen a few hours previously.

The next day, the ambulance crew found Fred Quilt and the others at the residence on the Anaham Reserve where they had been released by the two constables the night before. The paramedics examined Fred and they concluded he was in immediate need of medical attention. They were preparing to take him to Williams Lake but he refused to ride in the ambulance because there was the body of a dead infant in the vehicle. All attempts to talk him into the ambulance were futile and at last they decided to allow him to remain where he was.

Fred Quilt's refusal to ride in that ambulance was quite understandable. Many Native people are extremely superstitious about dead bodies, believing spirits or demons from the dead will possess them if they remain anywhere nearby. This belief was prevalent in all the Native groups or tribes I dealt with in my home district of Alberta and most definitely among the Chilcotin, Carrier and Shuswap people who I became familiar with during my police service in BC. As a policeman I attended sudden death situations at reserve communities where I was unable to find a single living person in the entire area. We frequently had to arrange for the removal of the body and return on another occasion when the population felt it was safe to come back to their homes. The second trip to these reserves was necessary to obtain detailed statements and any other

# THE FRED QUILT FRAME-UP

available evidence about the cause and circumstances of the death and to facilitate the routine coroner's inquiry or inquest.

The following day another ambulance and crew attended from Williams Lake and they stopped at the Anaham Reserve only to learn that Fred Quilt and his family had gone back to the Stone Reserve. The crew then drove to the Stone Reserve where they found Fred at his home; their examination showed him to be in dire need of medical attention. He was immediately taken to the hospital in Williams Lake. During the ambulance trip from Stone Reserve to the Williams Lake hospital, Fred told the attendant that a policeman had drug him out of his truck and jumped on him. The attendant was called at two subsequent inquests where he gave evidence about what Fred Quilt had told him about the alleged police brutality; the attendant also stated that he clearly recalled Fred saying that, "Christine had told him to tell that story." This attendant's evidence will have raised doubts in the minds of the juries at both inquests and as this story unfolds it becomes clear that this doubt was valid.

Fred Quilt died on November 30, 1977, within a day of being admitted to the hospital in Williams Lake. He was 55 years old. The autopsy showed that he had died of acute peritonitis caused by a torn small intestine near its junction to the large intestine.

Shortly after Fred's death, the grieving widow and the other two passengers (her sister-in-law and son) accused the police of extreme brutality which they swore had resulted in his death. All three claimed to have seen Constable Daryl Bakewell pull Fred out of the truck and then jump on him as he lay on the ground. Fred had made a similar accusation against the police to the ambulance crew and to hospital staff prior to his death. These allegations of extreme police violence from the deceased and the three surviving witnesses led to an investigation, two inquests and media attention about alleged police brutality unparalleled in the entire history of the Royal Canadian Mounted Police.

Native rights leaders from across the country and the USA flocked to Williams Lake and the Chilcotin to assist the victims of this alleged extreme police violence. All of these people came forward at the outset to support the Chilcotin Natives in what was reported and appeared to be a vicious and unjustifiable attack on a Native man. They formed the "Fred Quilt Committee" and issued a steady stream of media releases during the two inquests at Williams Lake and Kamloops. My experience over the years and my understanding of the reactions by people in stressful situations leads me to believe that as this saga unfolded, even these committee members, from the vantage point of their inside access, must have experienced doubt in the testimony at a minimum, but complete disbelief as a more likely reality. In spite of this, they all carried on with their questionable position to the end.

I was serving in Lytton at the time. From the moment the

## THE FRED QUILT FRAME-UP

accusations were made, panic spread throughout the RCMP's rank and file in British Columbia. "Was there any truth to the allegations?" even we had to wonder. Such actions were certainly totally out of character for the two dedicated members many of us had served with, met or knew by reputation.

The officer in charge of Kamloops sub-division automatically became the leader and decision-maker in the course of the investigation. All police actions around the Quilt case were under his command from the administrative district headquarters at Kamloops. Special investigators were called into the matter and they began to prepare for a coroner's inquest. All efforts at investigating the incident were blocked by the actions of the Fred Quilt Committee; this group had instructed all Natives who had been involved in any way to refuse any and all contact with police investigators. The investigators tried to take statements from the wife of the deceased, Christine Quilt, and the other two who were with them in the truck on the night of the incident but they were completely "stonewalled" by these three Native witnesses and all others who were less directly involved.

Written statements were eventually provided to the police by the Fred Quilt Committee. The three statements were nearly identical, very brief and made only one point, "The cop pulled Fred out of the truck and jumped on him."

The statements were recorded under very questionable

methods and circumstances. All three of the direct witnesses were allowed to remain together in the same room while their statements were recorded. A very basic investigational procedure was flagrantly disregarded by having these people together for the preparation of their statements. None of the Native rights people who obtained these statements were qualified as investigators in any way. With a trained investigator among them, the witnesses would have been separated while providing their stories and perhaps the false allegations would have been stopped at that early stage of the process.

In my years of police work I learned that three people never see and describe the same happening in the same way and with the same words. When an experienced investigator is confronted with three nearly identical descriptions of an event, there will be an immediate suspicion of collusion and much additional investigation will be required. Strangely, but entirely in keeping with the sensitivities, policies and methods of those times, this breach of basic investigative procedure was not given more than passing comment by the lawyers who acted for the Crown at both inquests. In spite of extreme doubts about the statements, there was nothing more to work with so they were presented at the inquests by these witnesses as written.

The first inquest began hearing evidence at Williams Lake

## THE FRED QUILT FRAME-UP

on January 13, 1972, less than six weeks after the death of Fred Quilt. The hearing lasted three days.

The lawyers for the coroner and the two police officers tried repeatedly to obtain details of what the witnesses had seen but their efforts were remarkably unsuccessful. There was a clear tendency in that era to not apply severe cross-examination pressure to a Native witness due to their supposed inability to understand the nature of our court system. No further details could be persuaded out of the witnesses; the one-liner was repeated freely but absolutely nothing more.

The bulk of the damning evidence from the three main witnesses was directed toward Constable Daryl Bakewell and it was alleged to have happened after Fred Quilt was taken out of his truck and he was on the ground below the driver's door. The witnesses claimed Daryl had removed Fred from the cab of the truck when in fact it was Peter Eakins who did that. Peter was in uniform while Daryl was in civilian dress. After Peter had removed Fred from the driver's position he immediately went to the passenger side to remove the other three from the cab of the truck.

At both inquests the three Native witnesses who stated they had seen the brutal assault on Fred Quilt were gently questioned about how they were able to see the alleged incident when they were on the passenger side of the truck. The transcript of the Williams Lake inquest shows the witnesses were obviously very uncomfortable with this line of questioning but they simply stated that they had each seen the incident although they would not provide any detail as to exactly where they were sitting or standing when they had observed it. When they were asked about the impossibility of them each being able to see the incident from the opposite side of the vehicle they would fall back to their one-line statement that, "The cop drug Fred out of the truck and jumped on him."

Considerable benefit of doubt went to the Natives. They are a people of few words by their nature but the benefit was huge. The similarities in the statements and the obvious reluctance to provide even the most basic details must have created very considerable doubt in the minds of the jurors. The jury members were all Cariboo residents and they will have accepted the evidence about total intoxication in all the truck passenger witnesses. This situation must have left the original jury with a mind-boggling choice about who to believe: police and other whites, or Natives. The evidence from the ambulance attendant about Fred Quilts' statement that Christine instructed him about what to say will have also contributed to doubt for the jury. In addition, the consulting pathologist to the inquest, Dr. John Sturdy, testified that Fred Quilt's injuries "were not consistent with a kick or series of kicks."

The first inquest's jury verdict was that Quilt had died of

## THE FRED QUILT FRAME-UP

injuries of an unknown origin and there was no conclusive evidence of wrongdoing by the attending police.

Immediately after the first jury had made their decision, Christine Quilt's lawyer, Harry Rankin, made an issue of the alleged association between two of the jury members and the police. He indicated that one of the jury members had shared room and board at a home in Williams Lake with an RCMP member some years prior to this incident. Rankin's allegations were quickly picked up by the media and every news source in Western Canada made mention of it. The Fred Quilt Committee and other Native rights advocate groups presented written and vocal arguments and pleas to anyone who would listen. The ensuing flare-up in the media and among the general population put great pressure on the BC Government. The matter was raised by an opposition member in a session of the Provincial Legislative Assembly with direct questions about the association between the police and jury members.

The case had by then come to the attention of the news media all over North America and to some extent around the world. The detailed reporting of every fragment of information had become an infatuation with the press, radio and television. The RCMP office at Alexis Creek was receiving hate letters and similar telephone calls at all hours of the day and night. Two very surprising and divergent sources of inflammatory writings to and about the police were the United Church of Canada and the United Fisherman and Allied Workers Union. These two organizations generated a great amount of material about the alleged evils the police had done in this and other incidents.

In that era the jury selection for a coroner's inquest was routinely delegated to the police by the local coroner. A police constable working at the Williams Lake Detachment was charged with selecting the jury for the first inquest in the same manner and method as with every inquest in that part of British Columbia up to that time. The constable set out in the small community and found six suitable and available citizens to form the jury. This selection was done in the same manner and method that he had used in all previous occasions.

The outcry resulted in the inquest verdict being overruled by the Attorney General and a second inquest was ordered. The overturning of a verdict from a coroner's jury was very rare.

The second inquest began hearing evidence with a new jury on July 17, 1972 in Kamloops. Because the first jury selection had been criticized for being all male and all white, the Kamloops jury was carefully picked to include Natives and women and to avoid any suggestion that any of the jury members were pro-police. The atmosphere around the entire matter had reached an extreme to the extent that the jury selection was not left with the local police. Input to the jury selection process was invited from the local

# THE FRED QUILT FRAME-UP

Natives in Kamloops and the final selection was conducted by representatives of the government agent's office. Two of the six new jury members were status Native Indians from the Kamloops area. Curiously, a woman from Kamloops had been selected as a potential jury member; she had Canadian Native Indian status but she was a Caucasian married to a Native. This person was asked to step aside during the final jury selection and she agreed to do so without making any issue of the matter.

The inquest dragged on for ten days during which time the two unfortunate police officers were again subjected to a process which could only be described as horrendous. Lawyer Harry Rankin again represented the Quilt family. He vigorously cross-examined all the police and medical witnesses, but his attacks against Constables Bakewell and Eakins were vicious and personal. Rankin pummelled witnesses with accusations and tried forcefully to put words into their mouths – particularly the two ill-fated members. These two members experienced extreme stress from every possible source during the entire time of the Quilt affair but their experiences on the stand at the two inquests must truly have been "Hell on Earth."

Apparently, for his remarks that police didn't mind beating up an Indian, but they "didn't like to get caught," Rankin was later called before the discipline board of the BC Law Society.

WHEN GRAMPA WAS A MOUNTIE

Although he was threatened with disbarment, charges were ultimately dropped and he was allowed to carry on practicing.

The Kamloops and District Labour Council held a large meeting in Kamloops that coincided with the second Quilt inquest, seemingly to show their support for the Natives. Eight officials of the labour council took part in a placard-waiving demonstration outside the old Kamloops Court House, where the Quilt inquest was being held. This was only a minor addition to the awful atmosphere that Peter and Daryl had to face each day of the hearing. The Fred Quilt Committee constantly made inflammatory statements about the proceedings; they made it very clear that they would not support anything but a damning verdict against the police in general but most specifically against the two members directly involved. At this point in time it became abundantly obvious that the goals and objectives of the Fred Quilt Committee were not to get to the truth of this matter but to "get the police."

A sermon was delivered to the congregation of the Unitarian Church in Vancouver on the eve of the second inquest into the Quilt case. The preacher rambled on for the full time of the sermon about the plight of the Natives and their brutal domination by the white majority. He did not make a direct statement about the guilt of the two policemen in the Quilt case but his message was clearly pointed in that direction and it left very little room for doubt about his beliefs in the matter. This incident was another

# THE FRED QUILT FRAME-UP

clear indication of the poisonous atmosphere that prevailed against the two accused police officers, and the Canadian police in general.

The verdict in the second inquest was the same as at the first: there was no conclusive evidence of wrongdoing or criminal action by the police. Many observers felt that what both juries said, without putting it into words, was that the evidence of the main Native witnesses was simply not credible.

Our justice system is founded on the principal of justice for all and the right of the accused to a fair and unbiased trial. Tragically there is no human made system that can meet such an onus in every situation. This weakness was clearly demonstrated in this incident where Constables Daryl Bakewell and Peter Eakins were figuratively "drawn and quartered" in the public view. The treatment dealt these two men during these two inquests was disgraceful. They were subjected to extreme and unwarranted punishment at the hands of the same system that claimed to be fair and just to all. Having chosen to serve their country as police officers they found themselves under a great cloud of suspicion even before the inquests began. The media, the judiciary, civil rights groups, the whole variety of Native rights groups, police haters, the United Church, some unions, and even a few fellow members of their own police organization contributed to a poisonous atmosphere which damaged both of these men to such an extent that they would never fully recover. Daryl Bakewell who had volunteered to assist his friend and co-worker took the brunt of the abuse.

At the original (Williams Lake) inquest, the questions presented by lawyers who represented the Native faction to the police witnesses were detailed and harsh. The three main Native witnesses were not pressured about their doubtful statements to nearly the same extent. I do not believe there was any conspiracy or plan to this. The imagined need for "political correctness" was still in its infancy at that time but it played a very damaging roll in the overall result of these two inquests. Had some or all of the Native witnesses been verbally badgered in a manner even slightly similar to the methods applied to the police witnesses, there may have been a very different verdict. Had any of Christine's disciples broken under the stress of an appropriate cross examination and confessed to their conspiracy this tragedy would have ended at that moment.

The two constables were again, at Kamloops, found to be not criminally responsible for the injuries that led to Fred Quilt's death. This verdict by the inquest juries was of little comfort to the two officers. Constable Peter Eakins was not directly accused by the Native witnesses and therefore the jury findings were perhaps more fitting to his situation. Constable Daryl Bakewell was directly accused of extremely violent and criminal acts by the Native witnesses. The "no conclusive evidence" verdicts by

# THE FRED QUILT FRAME-UP

the coroner's juries were therefore still extremely damning to him – to such an extent that he was never able to overcome the psychological effects of it.

The jury at Kamloops was misled by the Native witnesses and their counsels to such an extent that they concluded that the injury to Fred Quilt had happened between the time he was removed from his truck and when he was placed in the police vehicle. This finding indicated that the injury to Quilt had happened during the brief time he was in the care and custody of Constable Bakewell. Daryl knew without doubt that the injury did not happen at the time the jury believed, but he was unnecessarily left to carry blame until his own untimely death.

The finding by the Kamloops coroner's jury was, to Daryl, very similar to a verdict of *not guilty* in a criminal trial. Every experienced police officer knows that there is a vast difference between genuine innocence and a verdict of not guilty. A verdict of not guilty is a wonderful and positive thing for murderers, robbers, rapists and other perverts, but Daryl was a policeman. A court finding of not guilty has, in many situations, little or nothing to do with the truth and facts of a trial or inquest; all too often such a finding is due to the court's rules of evidence or admissibility of evidence or even seemingly trivial administrative details. All these technicalities, rules and regulations can most certainly be justified in the minds of the lawyer-dominated court system but my concern lies where there is disregard and exclusion of the hard truth and facts of a case. (An example of my concerns in this regard came in a recent case where the learned judge ruled that the police lacked the complete knowledge of prior drug involvement by a suspect before their suspicions were aroused by the very nervous actions of the suspect which prompted the use of their drug sniffing dog. The dog immediately found a large quantity of narcotics in the suspect's vehicle. The evidence of the drug find was ruled as not admissible because of inadequate prior knowledge on the part of the police investigators. The charges were dismissed.)

The juries in both inquests were presented with an extremely difficult situation and I am convinced that they did their very best to deal with it within the rules that governed them. In this case Daryl and Peter deserved a great deal more than the juries were able to provide and they were left to live with the extreme injustice of it until their deaths in November of 1991 and October of 2006.

A news story in the *Vancouver Province* newspaper on August 5, 1972 told of the acceptance of the jury findings at the Kamloops inquest by the Union of B.C. Indian Chiefs. The story said that the Chiefs were not totally satisfied with the result but they were prepared to live with it. Several members of the Union of B.C. Indian Chiefs had attended both inquests and had listened

# THE FRED QUILT FRAME-UP

carefully to all the evidence prior to their decision to accept the inquest findings. I believe that the acceptance of the jury verdict, by these men, is an indication that some or all of them had seen the weakness in the testimony provided by the Native witnesses and they had begun to doubt that evidence.

## Christine Quilt's Confession

Over the following years, rumors began to circulate in the Alexis Creek area that Christine Quilt had told others that she had lied about the injury to her husband. Corporal Jack Hest returned to the Alexis Creek area to investigate these rumors but nothing solid could be gathered from the usual sources in the community. Several people who were interviewed did indicate that there was talk among the Natives that the story put forward by Christine Quilt and the others was a fabrication. No hard evidence was available and the two accused policemen remained under the cloud of suspicion.

In the last days of September of 1976, Christine Quilt lay dying of cervical cancer in the Williams Lake hospital; death was nearby and Christine knew this. She was 47 years old.

A woman of Chilcotin Indian ancestry who worked at the hospital was able to speak and understand the Chilcotin language. This lady had left her home area in the Chilcotin to live in Williams Lake where she had found work at the hospital and

# WHEN GRAMPA WAS A MOUNTIE

had become a valuable asset to the staff and management of the Williams Lake hospital. During the days Christine spent in the hospital, this lady was frequently called on to interpret medical information to Christine and to translate any responses from her for the doctors and nurses. Christine was gravely ill and in her diminished capacity she believed she was receiving visitations with previously deceased relatives. These mystery visitors were pressuring Christine to atone for her past wrongdoing and thereby enable her to escape an eternal purgatory. Christine Quilt told her interpreter a strange story about how she had accidentally run over her husband with their truck and had lied at the inquests and encouraged others to back up her lies in order to smear the police and embarrass the dominant white society. The interpreter repeated this story to other staff at the hospital – among them was an acquaintance of Constable Francis "Frank" Boyle who was then stationed at Kamloops. This person made contact with Frank late in January 1977 and she told him what she had heard from both the deceased and the woman who acted as her interpreter.

Frank Boyle arranged an immediate flight by police aircraft to Williams Lake. He was accompanied by Staff Sergeant William "Bill" Sparks who was in charge of Kamloops general investigation section at that time. The two policemen attended at the hospital and other locations in the Williams Lake area where they obtained detailed statements about the confessions of Christine Quilt.

# THE FRED QUILT FRAME-UP

Apparently Christine Quilt had told a number of people she had lied about the injuries Fred Quilt had suffered which led to his death. She admitted she had accidentally backed their truck onto Fred and that he had severe abdominal pain after that until his death. The truck incident had happened shortly before and at the same location where Constables Eakins and Bakewell were to come in contact with them. Immediately after Peter and Daryl released the four people at the Anaham Reserve, Christine fabricated a story that one of the policemen had jumped on Fred. Christine then returned to their truck with two young men from the Anaham Reserve and they burned it to destroy any evidence of her having backed into and over her husband. These two accomplices gave evidence to support Christine's fabrications at both inquests.

Christine Quilt also confessed to the same people that she had shot and killed Rose Setah, another Native woman who lived on the Stone Reserve until her murder in 1968. Rose was alleged to have had a romantic connection to Fred Quilt.

The shooting was done during a potlatch celebration on the Stone Reserve which left the police to piece the incident together from the blurred knowledge of a group of witnesses who had all been totally intoxicated at the time of the murder. During the investigation Christine had provided a witness statement to the police, and later gave evidence at a preliminary hearing and at the

WHEN GRAMPA WAS A MOUNTIE

following murder trial, that Stephen Hink had deliberately shot Rose Setah and that she had seen it happen. Stephen Hink was so drunk at the time that he had no memory of the alleged offence and he later believed he may well have been guilty. He was convicted of manslaughter on the strength of Christine Quilt's evidence.

Apparently to clear her conscience further, Christine also told hospital staff and her interpreter about having shot cattle on several ranches in the vicinity of her home on a number of occasions. These incidents had been reported to the police but there was never any evidence available to associate these crimes to a specific person.

The news of the dying woman's confession spread rapidly within the RCMP. Chief Superintendent Gordon Dalton oversaw the production of a detailed report for the Attorney General of British Columbia, and presented a press release at a Vancouver news conference on March 17, 1977. Although there were front page stories the next day in many Canadian papers, the coverage by the media was far less extensive than it was for the original allegations and two inquests, and there was little mention of the extensive perjuries viciously attacking the two policemen.

From the Vancouver *Province* newspaper of March 18, 1977: "The new information is that Quilt was urinating behind the pick-up when his wife 'backed up the truck and knocked him down,'

# THE FRED QUILT FRAME-UP

said Dalton. 'Then she put Fred back in the cab of the truck before the RCMP arrived and rest, as they say, is history.' "

The United Church of Canada, the United Fishermen and Allied Workers Union, the Kamloops and District Labour Council, the Unitarian Church of Vancouver, and the Fred Quilt Committee and many others were all very obvious in their complete lack of motivation to now provide the truth to the masses. Likely these organizations and many of the witnesses at the inquests were embarrassed about their earlier actions and they did not wish to generate attention. If they were not embarrassed, they most certainly should have been. Their inaction itself is a very strong indication that all these people had rallied not in a quest for justice but to attack the police. Peter and Daryl were thrust into this travesty by fate alone; the same or similar fate awaited whichever policemen had answered the call of duty on that November night in 1971.

The media's relatively modest coverage of Christine Quilt's admission of perjury is still having a damaging effect to this day. Each time there is a suggestion of mistreatment of a Native by the police or any authority figure in Canada, the Quilt case is again raised to the fore. An example of this is a report in a Kamloops newspaper printed in April of 2006. The reporter was writing about the soon-to-be-demolished, historic Kamloops court house and highlighted the many historic trials that had been held in this grand old building. The article mentions the Quilt inquest and

209

WHEN GRAMPA WAS A MOUNTIE

says that Fred Quilt died after an alleged beating by members of the Royal Canadian Mounted Police. Had the actual cause of his death been given proper publicity in 1977, this reference would have been presented with an entirely different slant. The dying confessions of Christine Quilt are not generally known, even among our Native population, or else their activists would not still be so inclined to mention the Fred Quilt allegations at every opportunity.

As recently as January 19, 2008, a publication from a Vancouver law firm made references to the Fred Quilt case; the articles were about the questionable death of a Native man on the streets of Vancouver and they cited the Quilt incident as an example of brutality to the Natives by the police. If the mass media had shown more interest in the Christine Quilt confession and given it greater coverage, there would be no continuing references to this matter by those who feel a need to further discredit the RCMP or any other police organization.

Tragically, there are numerous incidents where Natives have died in police custody, most from alcohol or drug overdosing but some from other causes and no doubt better care and facilities could possibly have prevented some of these deaths. A number of these cases could be raised as examples if activists and lawyers feel the need to do so. The Fred Quilt case most certainly does not belong in that category.

# THE FRED QUILT FRAME-UP

Christine Quilt was obviously the leader of the conspiracy to blame the police for the death of her husband. This woman seems to have wielded considerable power among her peers and in her society in general. In a very brief time she convinced five or more people to commit perjury and each of these people willfully carried on with this plot throughout the two inquests. Close examination of the entire perjured story and the analysis of it through two inquests leads to the conclusion that the lying witnesses held greater fear or reverence for Christine Quilt than they did of conscience, decency and the Canadian justice system.

Christine Quilt was a person who was able to inflict her will on the minds and lives of many people around her. I imagine that had she lived her life before the arrival of the invading white settlers she may well have been a shaman or medicine-man among her people. She was a strong-willed person who stopped at nothing to have her way. Although Christine seemed to harbour a great hatred for the white conquerors of her homeland, the Setah murder indicates another facet of her mind-set. In that case Christine caused the death to one of her own people and grievous injustice to another, and she carried this secret with her for years. She clearly demonstrated a very clever understanding of the justice systems of the dominant society and was capable and willing to manipulate that system to accomplish her own evil purposes.

Immediately after the press release of the death-bed

211

confession by Christine Quilt, there was considerable media coverage directed toward the urgent need for Stephen Hink to be exonerated. The mass media broadcasted and printed quotes from senior police officers and from the Attorney General of British Columbia concerning the steps being taken to rectify the wrongful conviction of Hink. This was an example of the proper course of action in such a situation. Stephen Hink had been the victim of a great injustice perpetrated by Christine Quilt. He definitely deserved to be exonerated at the first opportunity. He was cleared of any wrongdoing surrounding the death of Rose Setah by the granting of a 'Royal Prerogative of Mercy' within a few months of the RCMP confession report.

The Fred Quilt saga began with a drunken accident but was deliberately turned into a savage attack against two innocent men. Perjury, obstruction of justice, counselling an offence and conspiracy offences were committed in abundance and were made very obvious by the death-bed confession of Christine Quilt. In spite of these facts there was an obvious lack of will from the Attorney General of BC or any other person in a position of authority to correct the corrupted findings of the two inquests on behalf of Peter Eakins and Daryl Bakewell.

While there was proper and correct willingness within our justice system to obtain a prompt exoneration for Stephen Hink who was another victim of this woman, nothing was done to

## THE FRED QUILT FRAME-UP

restore the reputations of the two RCMP constables. There were no moves toward re-opening of the inquest or any other positive action to clear these two police victims. I believe criminal charges should have been pressed against the witnesses who lied at both inquests to support the savage allegations of Christine Quilt. Certainly any of the direct witnesses could have ended this travesty by telling the truth at any point during either of the inquests. They all told their lies under oath and stuck with their stories through the minimal cross-examination at both the Williams Lake inquest and again at Kamloops. These liars include the two young men Christine Quilt took with her when she returned to their truck and set fire to it to destroy any evidence of her backing over her husband. Were Daryl and Peter somehow less worthy of justice than Stephen Hink because they chose to serve their country as peace officers? Were the lying witnesses somehow more deserving of an exemption from the criminal law than these two dedicated policemen were deserving of justice?

Both Peter and Daryl lived for a number of years after the Christine Quilt confessions and there is some comfort in knowing these two men did learn of the confession and that some records were created to at least partially clear their names and reputations. Nevertheless they were left to live with the inaction of our justice system to fully and properly exonerate them of any wrongdoing.

Another victim of the actions and inactions by many people

surrounding this tragedy was the simple "truth". Too many people were too ready to make conclusions and take actions without first looking realistically at every facet of the entire story.

Born at Quill Lake, Saskatchewan on July 12, 1946, **Daryl Wayne Bakewell** joined the Royal Canadian Mounted Police on October 7, 1966 at Calgary, Alberta. Daryl had been posted at Chase, Vernon and Lumby (all in BC) before Alexis Creek.

Daryl was transferred to Golden, BC immediately after the completion of the second inquest at Kamloops. I was stationed there at the time and had the pleasure of working with him. Soon after his arrival in Golden, Daryl found room and board with a local family and was soon treated by them as a family member. Daryl was a steady and reliable policeman who exercised skill and common-sense in every aspect of his duty. Like all of us he had strengths and weaknesses which he recognized in himself perhaps in a better way than many of us. Daryl enjoyed the thrill and excitement of fast driving so the high-powered police cars of those times were a joy to him. He was a very skillful driver, an ability which became very important to me in a story I have told in my first book. In that situation he handled our car in a way that allowed us to remove a very dangerous and suicidal driver from the highway without injuries to anyone.

I did not know Daryl before the Quilt incident. Prior to the

## THE FRED QUILT FRAME-UP

life-shattering experience of those vicious and unjust accusations, fierce inquest cross-examinations and intense media attention, Daryl had been known as a quiet man who enjoyed a close circle of friends. Those who he came to regard as friends were very important to him. His friends from before the Quilt incident who came to visit him at Golden were shocked at the change in his attitude and conduct. Whenever some of these friends from his past came to visit, Daryl wanted to immediately get somewhere where liquor was available and he drank greedily until he was intoxicated. This conduct was a very obvious change from the man they had known. Today we would refer to Daryl's condition as post-traumatic stress disorder. In those days, a member was expected to "be a man" and get on with work, and not show any weakness.

While I served with him, Daryl was extremely nervous about having police contact with Native Indians but this did not create problems of any consequence for us at Golden because there were almost no resident Natives within 80 kilometres. The care and consideration of the regional RCMP management was obvious in his posting to Golden, one of the few locations in the Kamloops district with a very small Native population. There were some citizens of Golden who had Native ancestors but they were far removed from the Native lifestyle and traditions. These people took an active part among the local population and were as much a part

215

# WHEN GRAMPA WAS A MOUNTIE

of the community as anyone else. I recall an incident one evening where one of the other policemen had arrested an impaired driver on the Trans-Canada Highway and had brought him to the Golden office for a breathalyzer test. The suspect was a Native Indian from another area of the province and Daryl was the breathalyzer operator on duty at the time. He called me at home and asked if I would attend at the office and conduct the test. I had enjoyed some wine with our evening meal and therefore could not properly conduct a breathalyzer test because the consumption of any alcohol immediately diminishes or extinguishes one's ability to smell alcohol on another person's breath. Because of this, I asked Daryl to do the test himself as he would for any other suspect. He was obviously reluctant but then handled the matter with the same skill and confidence as he did all other duties.

Daryl voluntarily left the RCMP on August 31, 1975. By that time he was drinking excessively but he always presented himself for duty clean and sober, and totally fit for whatever the shift might require of him. His faith and pride in the Force had been severely damaged by the Quilt affair and he felt it best to get away from it at that time.

I lost contact with Daryl after he left the force at Golden but the records show that on January 18, 1978 – ten months after the Christine Quilt confessions were reported – he rejoined the

216

## THE FRED QUILT FRAME-UP

RCMP. He was immediately posted to Punnichy, Saskatchewan. Punnichy is the detachment responsible for policing one of the largest Native Indian reserves in Canada. I am totally unable to comprehend how this man could logically have been stationed at a place like Punnichy after his devastating experience with Native people at Alexis Creek and his obvious reluctance to be in further contact with them. I can only speculate that some warped individual in the staffing branch took it upon himself to instigate a "make or break" posting and that no one in the remainder of the organization was caring, cautious or thoughtful enough to raise the issue and try to have it corrected. Surely in a police organization the size and breadth of the RCMP in all of Canada; a more suitable posting could have been found where this man's talents could have been well utilized without placing him in such a situation. However, in spite of this one very difficult posting, Daryl performed well and was promoted to corporal on October 21, 1982.

The last information I heard about Daryl was that he had been invalided to pension from the RCMP on July 9, 1987 and that his drinking was out of control. He had been in alcohol detoxification programs but he had not been able to overcome it. He died of the effects of long term and excessive alcohol abuse at Calgary, Alberta on November 14, 1991 at the age of forty-five years.

## WHEN GRAMPA WAS A MOUNTIE

**Peter David Eakins** remained in the RCMP service until his retirement in July of 2000. He and his family were transferred around the province in the manner common to all of us in the force during those times. Peter was promoted to the rank of staff sergeant in the final years of his service. He was diagnosed with leukemia in June of 2006 and he died in October of that year.

Peter was born in Maidstone, Kent, England in 1945. His parents were with the Canadian forces and were stationed there at that time. The family returned to Canada when Peter was two years old and he was raised and educated in Vancouver. Peter joined the RCMP in January of 1965. He met his wife-to-be in Prince Rupert, and he and Karen were married there in 1968. They were transferred to Alexis Creek in July 1970.

Peter and Karen were very active in all of the communities they were posted to. During their time in Alexis Creek they were foster parents to four Native children ranging in age from ten years to six months. Karen clearly recalls the concern and anguish each time one of these children was returned to their parental homes; how the Eakins household was saddened by the loss of a young person who had become part of their lives. Peter started the Boy Scouts program on the Anaham Reserve and was the chairman of the citizens group in Alexis Creek that obtained and installed the equipment necessary to bring television to the isolated community.

# THE FRED QUILT FRAME-UP

## STORY DEDICATION

This story is dedicated to the memories of two great Canadian men who served Canada and the citizens of Canada in an exemplary manner:

R.C.M.P. Regimental #23794 Peter David Eakins – served from 1965 to 2000

R.C.M.P. Regimental #25162 Daryl Wayne Bakewell – served from 1966 to 1975 and 1978 to 1987

I wish to say thank-you to the following persons who assisted me with my research during the writing of this story:

William Barry BEAULAC, Francis BOYLE,

Susan CROSS, Karen EAKINS, Ron FAIRHURST,

Nancy HANNUM, John J. HEST,

Monica LAMB-YORSKI, Dennis MacKAY,

William POOLER, Jan SOLOSTH and

Clifford SPENCE.

## The Author

CHARLES SCHEIDEMAN was born and grew up on a farm near Stony Plain, Alberta; he joined the RCMP when he was 21. After training in Ottawa, he served in seven BC communities until his retirement in 1989. He then worked another eight years for the provincial government in Victoria, where he still lives with his wife, Patricia. They have three children and five grandchildren — to whom this book is dedicated by their proud Grampa.

May 1968, Constable Charles Scheideman with a standard issue model 10 Smith & Wesson .38 Special.

Manufactured by Amazon.ca
Bolton, ON